Violet Ross

Awakened Soul Archetype
Mysteries of the Pleroma

Original Title: Arquétipo da Alma Desperta - Mistérios do Pleroma

Copyright © 2025, published by Luiz Antonio dos Santos ME.
This book is a work of non-fiction that explores Gnostic wisdom and spiritual awakening. Through an in-depth approach, the author provides insights into the mysteries of the Pleroma, the concept of Barbelo, and the path to higher consciousness and self-realization.

1st Edition
Production Team
Author: Violet Ross
Editor: Luiz Santos
Cover Design: Studios Booklas / Ethan Carter
Consultant: Sophia Reynolds
Researchers: Daniel Everett, Helena Morris, James Whitman
Layout Design: Marcus Flynn
Translation: Isabelle Thompson
Publication and Identification
Awakened Soul Archetype - Mysteries of the Pleroma
Booklas Publishing, 2025
Categories: Spirituality / Gnosticism / Esoteric Philosophy
DDC: 299.932 / **CDU:** 133.9
All rights reserved to:
Luiz Antonio dos Santos ME / Booklas Publishing

No part of this book may be reproduced, stored in a retrieval system, or transmitted in any form—electronic, mechanical, photocopying, recording, or otherwise—without prior written permission from the copyright holder.

Summary

Index Sistematic 5
Prologue 11
Chapter 1 Journey in Search of Knowledge 16
Chapter 2 The Universe of Divine Emanations 21
Chapter 3 The First Emanation and the Primordial Mind 26
Chapter 4 The Divine Feminine Aspect 31
Chapter 5 The Essence of Reality 37
Chapter 6 Wisdom, Power, and Immortality 43
Chapter 7 The Cosmic Genesis 49
Chapter 8 Other Aeons 55
Chapter 9 The Link to Redemption and Ascension 60
Chapter 10 Gnostic Texts 66
Chapter 11 Symbolism and Iconography 72
Chapter 12 Contemporary Spirituality 78
Chapter 13 Clarifying Misconceptions 84
Chapter 14 The Return to the Pleroma 90
Chapter 15 Open Questions 96
Chapter 16 Preparing the Way 101
Chapter 17 Visualizing Light and Wisdom 108
Chapter 18 The Heart for the Divine Feminine 116
Chapter 19 Working with the Divine Light 123
Chapter 20 Expanding Perception and Intuition 130
Chapter 21 Doubts and Challenges 137

Chapter 22 Living the Principles in the Material World........... 145
Chapter 23 Honoring the Divine Feminine............................... 153
Chapter 24 The Gnostic Community 161
Chapter 25 Deepening the Connection 168
Chapter 26 Model for Inner Transformation............................. 174
Chapter 27 Western Spirituality... 180
Chapter 28 Other Emanations 188
Chapter 29 Returning to the Source 196
Epilogue 201

Index Sistematic

Chapter 1: Journey in Search of Knowledge - Explores the fundamental principles of Gnosticism and its unique approach to the pursuit of spiritual understanding.

Chapter 2: The Universe of Divine Emanations - Unveils the structure of the universe according to Gnostic cosmology, emphasizing a hierarchy of spiritual dimensions and the concept of emanation from a transcendent Primordial Source.

Chapter 3: The First Emanation and the Primordial Mind - Delves into the mystery of Barbelo as the first emanation of the Divine Source, highlighting her role as the manifestation of the Primordial Mind and the foundation of the spiritual cosmos.

Chapter 4: The Divine Feminine Aspect - Explores the significance of the Divine Feminine in Gnostic thought, emphasizing its active and creative role in the cosmos and its importance for spiritual awakening.

Chapter 5: The Essence of Reality - Discusses the Gnostic perspective on the nature of reality, highlighting the concept of divine light as the essential substance of existence and the role of Barbelo in its manifestation.

Chapter 6: Wisdom, Power, and Immortality - Examines the key attributes of Barbelo, focusing on her embodiment of Divine Wisdom, Creative Power, and eternal life, and their implications for the Gnostic journey.

Chapter 7: The Cosmic Genesis - Explores Barbelo's active participation in the creation of the Pleroma, emphasizing her co-creative role alongside the Ineffable Father and her function as the divine matrix of spiritual emanations.

Chapter 8: Other Aeons - Introduces other important Aeons in Gnostic cosmology, highlighting their relationships with Barbelo and their roles in the divine realm, emphasizing the interconnection and harmony within the Pleroma.

Chapter 9: The Link to Redemption and Ascension - Discusses Barbelo's role as a link between humanity and the Pleroma, guiding souls toward redemption and spiritual ascension through Gnosis and the awakening of the divine spark within.

Chapter 10: Gnostic Texts - Delves into the ancient Gnostic scriptures that mention Barbelo, exploring their symbolism, interpretations, and significance for understanding her role in Gnostic cosmology and spirituality.

Chapter 11: Symbolism and Iconography - Explores the rich symbolism and iconography associated with Barbelo, analyzing visual symbols like the mirror and the image, and discussing the challenges of representing her transcendent nature.

Chapter 12: Contemporary Spirituality - Examines the relevance of Barbelo in contemporary spirituality, highlighting her appeal as a symbol of the Divine Feminine, her adaptability to diverse spiritual practices, and her potential to inspire personal transformation.

Chapter 13: Clarifying Misconceptions - Addresses common myths and misunderstandings surrounding Barbelo, refuting reductionist interpretations and emphasizing her unique position and importance within Gnostic cosmology.

Chapter 14: The Return to the Pleroma - Discusses the Gnostic journey as a path of return to the Source, highlighting the role of Barbelo as a guide and protector, and emphasizing the importance of Gnosis and direct spiritual experience in this process.

Chapter 15: Open Questions - Acknowledges the open questions and unresolved mysteries surrounding Barbelo, encouraging further exploration, contemplation, and openness to new discoveries on the spiritual journey.

Chapter 16: Preparing the Way - Emphasizes the importance of inner preparation for the Gnostic journey, highlighting principles such as pure intention, devotion, openness, ethics, inner stillness, and the creation of a sacred space.

Chapter 17: Visualizing Light and Wisdom - Explores the use of guided meditation and contemplation to connect with the divine light and wisdom of Barbelo, offering practical exercises to deepen the experience and integrate these qualities into daily life.

Chapter 18: The Heart for the Divine Feminine - Discusses prayer and invocation as tools for connecting with the Divine Feminine, offering examples inspired by Gnostic texts and encouraging the creation of personal prayers to deepen the relationship with Barbelo and the Supreme Mother.

Chapter 19: Working with the Divine Light - Explores techniques for channeling and integrating divine light into daily life, including conscious breathing, visualization, and the invocation of Barbelo as a channel for this transformative energy.

Chapter 20: Expanding Perception and Intuition - Emphasizes the importance of expanding perception and developing intuition in the Gnostic journey, offering practical exercises to transcend the limitations of the rational mind and connect with higher consciousness.

Chapter 21: Doubts and Challenges - Addresses the doubts, obstacles, and challenges that arise on the spiritual journey, offering strategies to overcome them with perseverance, patience, and self-compassion, guided by the support of Barbelo and the Supreme Mother.

Chapter 22: Living the Principles in the Material World - Discusses the integration of Gnostic principles into everyday life, offering practical examples of how to apply Gnostic wisdom in relationships, work, decision-making, and ethical conduct.

Chapter 23: Honoring the Divine Feminine - Explores ways to honor and celebrate the Divine

Feminine in Gnostic practice, including the adaptation of Gnostic rituals and ceremonies for contemporary use, with examples of rituals dedicated to Barbelo and the Supreme Mother.

Chapter 24: The Gnostic Community - Emphasizes the importance of community and mutual support in the Gnostic journey, offering suggestions for finding or creating Gnostic communities and highlighting the benefits of sharing the journey with other seekers.

Chapter 25: Deepening the Connection - Encourages the reader to continue deepening their connection with Barbelo and the Pleroma, exploring new practices, expanding consciousness, and embracing the continuous journey of spiritual growth and discovery.

Chapter 26: Model for Inner Transformation - Presents Barbelo as an archetypal model for inner transformation, inspiring the integration of feminine and masculine aspects, the awakening of consciousness, and the realization of the divine potential within each individual.

Chapter 27: Western Spirituality - Explores the influence of Gnosticism and the archetype of Barbelo on Western spirituality throughout history, discussing possible connections with Hermeticism, Kabbalah, Christian mysticism, and contemporary spiritual movements.

Chapter 28: Other Emanations - Introduces other important emanations and figures of the Pleroma, such as Christ, Sophia, Seth, the Demiurge, and the Holy

Spirit, highlighting their roles and significance within Gnostic cosmology.

Chapter 29: Returning to the Source - Concludes the book with a message of hope and inspiration, summarizing the main themes, reinforcing the importance of connection with Barbelo and the divine light, and encouraging the reader to continue their spiritual journey with perseverance and joy.

Prologue

In a society that shapes us from birth to believe in pre-fabricated truths, unquestionable dogmas, and limiting narratives, the flame of authentic seeking is often suffocated under the weight of mental domestication. We have been conditioned to accept what we have been taught, to follow pre-determined paths, and to conform to superficial answers. However, amidst the fog of imposed beliefs, the human soul still yearns for something more, for a truth that resonates with its essence, that answers its deepest existential questions, and that reveals its true role within creation.

For those who dare to question, who refuse to settle for superficial answers, and who feel the flame of inner seeking burning in their hearts, this book emerges as a map, a guide, and a source of inspiration. In its pages, we invite the reader to embark on a journey of rediscovery, to delve into the depths of ancient Gnostic wisdom, and to unravel the mystery of Barbelo, the First Emanation of the Divine Source, the archetype of the Divine Feminine, and the key to awakening higher consciousness.

Gnosticism, as a whole, represents an awakening of human consciousness beyond the limitations of the material world. More than a mere philosophy or religious system, it is configured as an intrinsic journey in search of knowledge, an ancestral thirst to understand the ultimate nature of reality and our place within it.

At the heart of Gnosticism lies the conviction that there is a higher knowledge, a "gnosis," capable of freeing the individual from the illusions and shackles of earthly existence. This knowledge is not limited to intellectual erudition or the accumulation of information. It is a deep and intuitive understanding of the truth, a revelation that transcends discursive reason and penetrates the realms of direct experience.

Gnosis is a saving knowledge, a path of enlightenment that leads to liberation from the cycle of suffering and ignorance that characterizes the human condition in this world. The Gnostic search for knowledge is not an escape from the world, but a courageous dive towards the truth, a recognition that the true homeland of the soul lies in a realm of light and perfection that transcends the limitations of the material universe.

The concept of Pleroma, the realm of divine fullness, and of the Primordial Emanation, the first manifestation of the Ineffable Source, is an ancient concept, present in various mystical and philosophical traditions. In Gnosticism, this concept gains a unique strength and clarity, revealing the structure of the divine universe, the hierarchy of the Aeons, the beings of light that emanate from the Source, and the path of return of the human soul to its original home.

The figure of Christ, as an Aeon that manifests in the material world, is also central to Gnosticism.

However, the Gnostic view of Christ differs from that presented in Orthodox Christianity. For the Gnostics, Christ is not the only begotten Son of God incarnate in the flesh, but an emissary of the Pleroma, an enlightened being who came to Earth to awaken the sleeping humanity and reveal the path of Gnosis.

Unfortunately, many of the original teachings of Christ and the Gnostics were distorted, suppressed, and even demonized throughout history. The need for control of the masses by religious and political institutions led to the creation of rigid dogmas, based on the fear of eternal punishment and submission to authority. The human mind has been domesticated, conditioned to believe blindly and to follow imposed dictates, stifling its ability to question, to seek the truth, and to awaken to its own divinity.

However, the flame of Gnosis has never been completely extinguished. Over the centuries, Gnostic wisdom has remained alive in mystical and esoteric currents, in hidden texts and oral traditions, awaiting the opportune moment to re-emerge and rekindle the flame of authentic seeking for the truth.

And this moment is now. In an increasingly complex, fragmented, and crisis-ridden world, ancient Gnostic wisdom is resurfacing with strength, offering an alternative to limiting dogmas, an answer to the thirst for knowledge, and a path to awakening higher consciousness.

This book aims to be a guide on this journey of rediscovery. In its pages, we explore the mystery of Barbelo, the first emanation of the Divine Source, the archetype of the Divine Feminine, and the key to understanding Gnostic cosmology and soteriology.

Barbelo, as the first manifestation of the Divine Mind, represents primordial wisdom, the light that illuminates the path back to the Pleroma, and the creative power that animates the universe. She is the Supreme Mother, the cosmic matrix from which everything emanates, the unconditional love that welcomes and nourishes the human soul on its journey back to the Source.

Throughout this book, we invite you to delve into the depth of Barbelo's symbolism, to explore her relationships with other important Aeons, to understand her role in creation and redemption, and to discover spiritual practices to connect with her energy, her wisdom, and her light.

Through the experience of Gnostic principles in daily life, you can awaken the divine spark within you, expand your consciousness, transcend the limitations of the material world, and walk the path back to the Pleroma, the realm of fullness and light.

This book is an invitation to those who dare to question, who seek the truth beyond dogmas, and who yearn for an authentic and transformative spiritual experience. It is a call to awaken your sleeping soul, to free yourself from the chains of mental domestication, and to assume your true role as co-creator of a reality more aligned with light, love, and divine wisdom.

May this book be a map on your journey of rediscovery, a guide in your search for Gnosis, and an inspiration to live the fullness of your divine potential.

May the light of Barbelo illuminate your path and may the love of the Supreme Mother accompany you every step of your journey.
    Luiz Santos
    Editor

Chapter 1
Journey in Search of Knowledge

The quest for transcendent knowledge is an innate impulse of humanity, a profound need to understand the ultimate nature of existence and the role of human beings in the vast fabric of the cosmos. Gnosticism, more than a philosophical or religious current, represents this restlessness in its most intense form, offering a vision of reality that transcends appearances and challenges conventional conceptions. Unlike knowledge acquired through reason and sensory experience, Gnostic wisdom is revealing and liberating, a key that enables the overcoming of illusions that limit the full understanding of being. This search for absolute truth is not just an intellectual exercise, but a path of inner transformation, in which the individual awakens to their own spiritual nature and recognizes the existence of a greater reality, hidden beneath the materiality of the visible world. At the heart of this journey is the conviction that the universe as we know it is not the definitive expression of divinity, but rather an imperfect manifestation, a distorted reflection of the true light that dwells beyond the limits of time and space.

Gnosticism emerged in a scenario of great cultural and spiritual effervescence, in the first centuries of the

Common Era, absorbing and re-signifying elements of diverse philosophical and religious traditions. Influences from Judaism, early Christianity, Platonism, and the mystery cults of the East converged to form a vast mosaic of teachings, the essence of which resided in the search for gnosis – the supreme knowledge that allows human beings to free themselves from the shackles of ignorance and suffering. This awakening process does not occur automatically or passively; it requires a conscious effort to transcend the limitations imposed by the material world and access the spiritual dimension of existence. Unlike institutional religions, which often emphasize faith in dogmas and hierarchical structures, Gnosticism proposes an individual path of discovery, in which each person must tread their own journey towards enlightenment. Thus, the Gnostic tradition not only presents itself as a body of beliefs, but as an invitation to inner exploration and reconnection with the divine origin, a crossing that leads to the recognition that the true essence of the human being belongs to a realm of fullness and light.

From this perspective, earthly existence takes on a paradoxical character: at the same time that it represents an imprisonment, it offers the opportunity for the awakening of consciousness. The material world, conceived as an imperfect creation of the Demiurge, is not the definitive home of the soul, but a transitory stage, a trial that impels the individual to seek their true spiritual destiny. This dualistic conception, which opposes matter and spirit, illusion and truth, structures Gnostic thought and gives it a deeply transformative character. It is not just a question about the nature of the universe, but a call to action – an invitation for each individual to recognize the divine spark that dwells within them and begin their journey of return to the Pleroma, the realm of supreme light. Thus, Gnosticism transcends the barriers of time and resonates with those who, regardless of the era in which they live, feel an inner longing for something beyond the superficial answers offered by the visible world. It is, in essence, a path of liberation, an awakening to the true reality that awaits beyond the shadows of the material world.

At the heart of Gnosticism lies the conviction that there is a higher knowledge, a "gnosis," capable of freeing the individual from the illusions and shackles of earthly existence. This knowledge is not limited to intellectual erudition or the accumulation of information. It is a deep and intuitive understanding of the truth, a revelation that transcends discursive reason and penetrates the domains of direct experience. Gnosis is a saving knowledge, a path of enlightenment that leads to liberation from the cycle of suffering and ignorance that characterizes the human condition in this world.

The relevance of Gnosticism persists to this day, resonating with those who feel a spiritual longing that goes beyond conventional answers. In a world marked by materialism, consumerism, and superficiality, Gnosticism offers a profound and challenging alternative. It invites us to question the premises of consensual reality, to probe the depths of our own consciousness, and to seek a higher meaning for our existence. The Gnostic search for knowledge is not an escape from the world, but rather a courageous dive towards the truth, a recognition that the true homeland of the soul is found in a realm of light and perfection that transcends the limitations of the material universe.

For the Gnostic, the world in which we live is not the ultimate manifestation of divine reality, but rather an imperfect creation, generated by a lower entity, the Demiurge, often identified with the figure of the God of the Old Testament from a specific interpretative perspective. This Demiurge, although powerful, is considered ignorant of the Primordial Divine Source, the true transcendent and ineffable God who resides in a realm of pure light, known as the Pleroma. The creation of the material world, in the Gnostic view, is the result of an error, a flaw in the divine emanation that resulted in the separation of the primordial light and the generation of darkness and matter.

Within this complex cosmology, humanity occupies a paradoxical position. Imprisoned in material bodies and immersed in a world of illusion and suffering, human beings nevertheless carry a divine spark, a fragment of the primordial light that yearns to return to its origin. This divine spark, also referred to as "pneuma" or "spirit," is our true essence, the part of us that is intrinsically connected to the Pleroma and that possesses the potential to awaken and achieve gnosis.

The Gnostic awakening implies recognizing our true spiritual identity and freeing ourselves from the shackles of ignorance and materialism that keep us trapped in the cycle of earthly existence. This awakening is not a passive event, but rather an active and transformative process that requires effort, introspection, and the search for knowledge. The Gnostic journey is an inner pilgrimage, a path of self-discovery that leads us back to the Divine Source, to the Pleroma of light and fullness from which we all emanate.

The Gnostic texts, discovered mainly in the Nag Hammadi library in Egypt in 1945, offer a fascinating glimpse into the richness and complexity of Gnostic thought. Gospels, apocrypha, acts, and epistles, among other textual genres, reveal an elaborate cosmology, a peculiar soteriology, and a profound yearning for transcendence. Texts such as the Gospel of Thomas, the Apocryphon of John, the Gospel of Mary Magdalene, and the Pistis Sophia, transport us to a symbolic and archetypal universe, where divine figures and cosmic entities interact in a cosmic drama of creation, fall, and redemption.

The study of Gnosticism is not just an academic foray into the past, but a living dialogue with a perennial spiritual tradition that continues to inspire and challenge our understanding of reality. By exploring Gnosticism, we open the doors to a new perspective on ourselves, the world, and the divine. We are invited to question our beliefs, to expand our consciousness, and to embark on a personal journey of seeking knowledge and spiritual liberation. The awakening of Gnosticism is, ultimately, an invitation to awaken to our own inner divinity and to reconnect with the Primordial Source of all existence.

Chapter 2
The Universe of Divine Emanations

The structure of the universe, according to the Gnostic perspective, is not limited to the material and visible domain, but extends to a higher reality, where the divine essence manifests itself in its fullness. Unlike cosmological conceptions that present creation as a single and deliberate act of a supreme entity, Gnosticism proposes a dynamic model of emanation, in which all things arise from a transcendent Primordial Source. This Source, ineffable and absolute, cannot be understood by the senses or by common reason, because its existence transcends any limited definition. In its fullness, it does not create arbitrarily, but continually radiates aspects of itself, forming a cosmos ordered by successive manifestations of its light. Thus, reality is not conceived as a closed and static system, but as a continuous flow of divine energy that permeates all levels of being. Gnostic cosmology, therefore, presents the universe as a hierarchy of spiritual dimensions, where divine emanations maintain an intrinsic connection with the original Source, even when progressively distant from its absolute perfection.

At the heart of this structure is the Pleroma, the realm of fullness where the purest manifestations of divinity dwell. This domain should not be confused with a physical space, but understood as a state of existence where perfection and divine light are fully expressed. The beings that make up the Pleroma, known as Aeons, are not independent entities in the traditional sense, but living aspects of the divinity itself, expressions of its eternal attributes. Each Aeon reflects an essential principle of the supreme reality, such as wisdom, truth, and love, and together they form the totality of the divine manifestation. This cosmic order, however, does not remain immutable. Within this continuous process of emanation, something occurs that breaks the harmony of the Pleroma, resulting in the separation between spiritual and material reality. This event, often described as a fault or an error in the divine manifestation, originates the physical world as we know it – an imperfect and limited creation, removed from the primordial light.

This rupture establishes a fundamental dualism in Gnostic cosmology, in which human existence takes place in a world that, although derived from the divine, is corrupted and marked by ignorance. The material universe is, therefore, not the definitive expression of reality, but a transitory domain, a shadow of the true fullness of the Pleroma. However, even in this state of separation, the divine spark is not completely extinguished. It remains hidden within creation, dormant within human beings, awaiting awakening to its true origin. This vision not only explains the structure of the cosmos, but also provides a purpose for existence: the return to the Source. Understanding this cosmic journey is essential to interpreting the role of Barbelo, the first emanation of the Divine Mind, whose presence inaugurates the process of manifestation and establishes the foundation for all subsequent spiritual order.

Creation, in the Gnostic perspective, is not a single and voluntary act of a personal God, but a dynamic and continuous process of emanation. From the Primordial Source, successive layers of divine reality emanate, each one less perfect and luminous than the previous one. These emanations are not separations from the Source, but rather manifestations of its fullness, like rays of light that radiate from a central sun. The Pleroma is a complex and interconnected hierarchy of Aeons, each representing an aspect or attribute of the primordial divinity.

At the top of this hierarchy, close to the Ineffable Source, are the highest Aeons, those that most directly reflect the divine perfection. As the emanation distances itself from the Source, the divine light becomes fainter and reality becomes less perfect, culminating in the creation of the material universe, a domain of darkness, ignorance, and suffering, radically separated from the Pleroma of light. This separation was not intentional, but rather the result of a disturbance, an imbalance in the process of emanation, which led to the generation of an imperfect cosmic entity, the Demiurge.

The Demiurge, often identified with the creator God of the Old Testament under a specific Gnostic lens, is considered the architect of the material world. Although powerful in his own domain, the Demiurge is ignorant of the Primordial Source and of the true divine nature. He believes himself to be the supreme God and demands worship from his creatures, keeping humanity in ignorance of its true origin and spiritual destiny. The material world, created by the Demiurge, is an imperfect and distorted imitation of the Pleroma, a realm of illusion and suffering that imprisons the divine spark present in human beings.

Within Gnostic cosmology, the Aeons play crucial roles. They are divine entities, manifestations of intelligence, love, wisdom, and other attributes of the Primordial Source. Each Aeon has a specific function within the divine economy, contributing to the harmony and fullness of the Pleroma. Some Aeons are responsible for aspects of creation, others act as mediators between the Pleroma and the material world, and still others play soteriological roles, assisting in the redemption and awakening of humanity.

It is important to note that Gnostic cosmology is not a static and rigid system, but rather a dynamic and fluid vision of divine reality. The relationships between the Aeons, the process of emanation, and the interaction between the Pleroma and the material world are complex and multifaceted themes, which vary among the different Gnostic schools. However, the central concept of a universe of divine emanations, originating from a transcendent Primordial Source and separated from the imperfect material world, remains constant.

The hierarchy of the Aeons in the Pleroma reflects the order and harmony of the divine realm. This hierarchy should not be understood as an oppressive power structure, but rather as a manifestation of the diversity and richness of the divinity. Each Aeon, however "lower" it may be in the hierarchy in relation to the Primordial Source, possesses its own beauty, importance, and function within the Pleroma. The totality of the Aeons, in their interconnection and harmony, composes the fullness of the Pleroma, the complete manifestation of the divinity.

The creation of the material universe, although seen as a fault or an error in the Gnostic perspective, is not an entirely negative event. Even within the world of matter and darkness, the divine spark persists, offering humanity the potential for awakening and redemption. Gnostic cosmology is not only a description of the structure of the universe, but also a map for the spiritual journey, a guide for the return of the soul to the Pleroma of light. Understanding Gnostic cosmology is fundamental to understanding the role of Barbelo within this system, as she occupies a unique place as the first emanation and manifestation of the Primordial Mind.

Chapter 3
The First Emanation and the Primordial Mind

At the heart of Gnostic cosmology, the first divine emanation represents the moment when the supreme reality begins to manifest, overflowing from its Ineffable Source to give rise to the Pleroma. This primordial instant is not a creation in the conventional sense, but a spontaneous externalization of the divine essence, a pure reflection of the Ineffable Father's primordial thought. The divinity, hitherto transcendent and unknowable, initiates its self-projection through a principle that carries within it the fullness of its light, wisdom, and creative power. It is in this context that Barbelo arises, not as a being separate from the Source, but as its first revelation, the manifestation that makes accessible the unfathomable depth of the Divine Mind. This first emanation not only reflects the totality of the Absolute but also inaugurates the cosmic structure upon which all other spiritual realities are organized. Barbelo, as the first expression of divinity, does not arise as a subordinate being, but as an essential aspect of the Ineffable Father himself, carrying within her the fullness of his thought and creative will.

By manifesting as the first emanation, Barbelo becomes the active principle that enables the structuring of the Pleroma, allowing the divine powers to flow in an orderly manner. Within this perspective, her existence is not an isolated event, but a fundamental link in the chain of cosmic emanation. Her presence establishes an axis through which the attributes of the Ineffable Father become operational, giving rise to the hierarchies of Aeons that make up the realm of divine fullness. In Gnostic thought, the idea of a first feminine principle plays a crucial role in the economy of the divine, since Barbelo not only reflects the totality of the divine mind but also embodies the generative aspect of spiritual creation. Her role is, therefore, twofold: as a manifestation of supreme thought, she represents absolute wisdom and primordial intelligence; as the matrix of subsequent emanations, she becomes the cosmic womb, the source from which the other aspects of divine reality emerge. In this way, Barbelo is not only a representation of the divine feminine but the very embodiment of the creative and ordering power of divinity.

The appearance of Barbelo within Gnostic cosmology marks the beginning of differentiation within absolute unity, a transition that allows the divinity to express its attributes without losing its ineffable essence. This initial emanation, however, does not imply a separation or rupture within the divine being, but a harmonious extension of its presence. Barbelo is the principle by which the invisible becomes perceptible, by which the transcendent becomes immanent without losing its infinite nature. Her existence points to the need to understand the divine not as an isolated and distant entity, but as a dynamic and interactive reality, which continually expands to manifest its own fullness. Through his connection with Barbelo, the Gnostic seeker is invited to reflect on his own spiritual origin and on the call to awakening. The soul's journey towards transcendent knowledge is not just a path of personal enlightenment, but a return to the primordial matrix from which everything originated.

To understand Barbelo is to understand the principle of divine manifestation and, consequently, the role that each spiritual spark plays within the great cosmic drama of redemption and return to the Source.

The importance of Barbelo transcends her position as the first emanation. She is considered the Primordial Mind in action, Divine Wisdom personified, the creative force that participates in cosmic genesis. In Gnostic texts, Barbelo is described with a variety of names and titles that reflect her multifaceted nature and her fundamental role in the divine economy. She is invoked as the "Immaculate Virgin," the original and untouched purity of divinity, the Triple Mother who encompasses the feminine and masculine aspects of the divine, the Image of the Invisible Father, and the Primordial Light that radiates from the Source.

Upon being revealed, Barbelo manifests the essential nature of the Ineffable Father, making visible the invisible, comprehensible the incomprehensible. She is the connecting link between the absolute transcendence of the Source and the manifestation of the

Pleroma, the bridge that allows the primordial divinity to express itself and communicate with its subsequent emanations. Through Barbelo, divine attributes such as wisdom, life, light, and power become operational and dynamic within the divine realm.

The description of Barbelo in Gnostic texts often evokes images of radiant light and sublime beauty. She is frequently associated with the figure of the "virgin of light," resplendent and pure, emanating a luminosity that illuminates the entire Pleroma. This image of the virgin should not be interpreted literally or restricted to a sexual connotation, but rather as a metaphor for the purity, integrity, and untouchability of the primordial divine essence, which remains immaculate and untainted by the creation of the imperfect material world.

As the Triple Mother, Barbelo embodies the totality of divinity, uniting within herself the masculine and feminine principles, the active and the passive, being and non-being. This threefold nature reflects the completeness and self-sufficiency of the primordial divinity, which contains within itself all potentialities and all manifestations. The designation of Triple Mother may also allude to her generative function within the Pleroma, being the source of emanation of other Aeons and the primordial matrix of divine creation.

In the various Gnostic texts, Barbelo assumes different roles and relationships with other Aeons, but her position as the first emanation and the manifestation of the Primordial Mind remains constant. In the Apocryphon of John, for example, Barbelo appears as the first manifestation of the Ineffable Father, the luminous response to primordial thought, the force that gives shape and reality to the divine archetypes. In the Gospel of Judas, she is presented as a central figure in divine cosmology, playing a crucial role in the creation and revelation of Gnostic knowledge.

The image of Barbelo, as conceived in Gnostic texts, challenges traditional representations of divinity, often centered on masculine and patriarchal figures. By placing the feminine figure of Barbelo at the center of divine cosmology, Gnosticism emphasizes the importance of the feminine principle, of wisdom, of intuition, and of the creative force that emanates from the divine. This emphasis on the divine feminine represents a distinctive and relevant aspect of Gnostic thought, which resonates particularly with contemporary spiritual sensibilities in search of a more balanced and inclusive vision of divinity.

To contemplate Barbelo is to contemplate the primordial face of divinity, the manifestation of the Primordial Mind in its original purity and power. She is the portal to Gnostic knowledge, the key that unlocks the doors to understanding the divine nature and our own spiritual potential. Through connection with Barbelo, we can glimpse the light of the Pleroma and begin the journey of return to the Source, awakening the divine spark that resides within us.

Chapter 4
The Divine Feminine Aspect

The essence of the divine cannot be limited to a single expression or attribute. In Gnosticism, this understanding manifests sublimely through the recognition of the feminine aspect of divinity, which is not merely complementary to the masculine principle, but equally fundamental and active in the process of creation and redemption. While many religious traditions emphasize the figure of a masculine creator God, relegating the feminine principle to a secondary or even non-existent role, Gnosticism elevates it to a level of primordiality, recognizing it as an indispensable element of the divine totality. This recognition is not merely symbolic or metaphorical, but expresses a profound cosmic reality, in which the creative and sustaining energy of the universe manifests in both the masculine and feminine principles, in perfect balance and harmony. The Supreme Mother, in her purest form, is not a divinity separate from the Absolute, but its active manifestation, the primary emanation that makes the existence and perpetuation of the spiritual cosmos possible.

Emerging as the first manifestation of the divine, the feminine principle expresses the fullness of wisdom and creative power inherent in the Primordial Source. In the Pleroma, this energy is not restricted to a passive role of receptivity, but presents itself as the very dynamism of emanation, the matrix through which reality expands and organizes itself. This aspect of the divine feminine, often associated with figures like Barbelo and Sophia, represents the consciousness of the Absolute itself as it reflects its light upon creation, enabling communication between the transcendent and the immanent. Thus, the Supreme Mother is not only the cosmic womb that gives rise to spiritual realities, but also the creative intelligence that orders and harmonizes all subsequent manifestations. Her existence reaffirms the notion that the true nature of the divine is not fragmented or unilateral, but integrates all polarities in an absolute balance, in which the feminine and the masculine do not compete, but coexist in perfect unity.

The recognition of the feminine principle as an inherent part of divinity has profound implications for Gnostic spirituality. It reframes the search for knowledge not only as a rational and analytical act, but as an intuitive and experiential process, in which the awakening of inner wisdom is as essential as intellectual understanding. This feminine aspect of spiritual awakening is reflected in the figure of the Supreme Mother as a guide and protector of those who seek gnosis, assisting in the recovery of the divine spark imprisoned in the material world. Through her, humanity is reminded of its true origin and its final destiny in the Pleroma, where the fullness of being manifests in the harmonious fusion of all aspects of divinity. Thus, by contemplating the divine feminine in Gnosticism, not only is a more complete and balanced view of the cosmos restored, but a path to spiritual reintegration is also opened, in which the totality of being can finally be recognized and experienced in its purest and most luminous form.

The importance of the divine feminine principle in Gnosticism manifests in various ways. First, the very Gnostic cosmology, with its emphasis on emanations from the Primordial Source, can be interpreted as a process of divine birth, where the Supreme Mother plays the role of cosmic matrix, giving birth to the myriad Aeons and realities that make up the Pleroma. This image of creation as emanation, as opposed to creation as an act of imposition or external design, highlights the organic, fluid, and nurturing nature of the divine feminine principle.

The Supreme Mother, as a representation of divine wisdom, is frequently identified with the figure of Sophia, Wisdom. Sophia, in Gnosticism, is not just an intellectual attribute, but rather a dynamic cosmic force, the creative intelligence that permeates the Pleroma and incessantly seeks knowledge of the Primordial Source. It is through Sophia's wisdom that divinity manifests and becomes knowable, and it is through the pursuit of wisdom that humanity can aspire to spiritual awakening.

Beyond wisdom, the Supreme Mother also embodies divine light, the radiant and primordial essence that emanates from the Source. This light is not merely physical, but rather a spiritual light, an energy of consciousness and truth that illuminates the path to the

Pleroma. The Supreme Mother, as the bearer and manifestation of this light, becomes a beacon of hope and a guide for those seeking spiritual redemption. Her light dispels the darkness of ignorance and illusion that obscures humanity's vision, revealing the true nature of divine reality.

Divine creative power is another fundamental aspect of the Supreme Mother. She is not only receptive and passive, but also active and dynamic, actively participating in the creation and maintenance of the universe. Her creative power manifests in the emanation of the Aeons, in the harmonious organization of the Pleroma, and even in the pursuit of redemption of the material world. The Supreme Mother is not only the source of wisdom and light, but also the driving force behind divine manifestation in all its forms.

Barbelo, as the first emanation of the Primordial Source, is understood as a direct and primordial manifestation of the Supreme Mother. She inherits and expresses the essential attributes of the divine feminine: wisdom, light, and creative power. Barbelo personifies the primordial feminine energy in its purest and most potent form, being the archetype of the Divine Mother for all subsequent emanations. Her connection to the primordial feminine energy establishes a divine standard, a model of balance and completeness that resonates throughout the Pleroma.

Barbelo's connection to the primordial feminine energy is not limited to the mere representation of divine attributes. It also manifests in her soteriological function, in her role in the restoration and redemption of humanity. In Gnosticism, humanity is seen as having been imprisoned in the material world, separated from its divine origin and immersed in ignorance and suffering. The Supreme Mother, through her emanations like Barbelo and Sophia, seeks to awaken the divine spark within humanity and guide it back to the Pleroma.

The role of the Supreme Mother in the restoration and redemption of humanity is multifaceted. She offers Gnostic wisdom, the liberating knowledge that reveals the true nature of reality and the path to salvation. She radiates divine light, dispelling the darkness of ignorance and illuminating the path of return. She nurtures and protects the divine spark within each individual, strengthening it and guiding it on its spiritual journey. The Supreme Mother is not just a distant and transcendent figure, but a loving and compassionate presence, actively engaged in the redemption of humanity.

The emphasis on the divine feminine principle in Gnosticism represents a profoundly transformative perspective in relation to patriarchal religious traditions. By elevating the Supreme Mother to a prominent place in the divine cosmology, Gnosticism challenges the hierarchies of power and structures of domination that have often characterized organized religions. It offers a more balanced and inclusive view of divinity, recognizing the importance of both the masculine and feminine principles in the manifestation of the divine.

The recognition of the Supreme Mother in Gnosticism is not just a theological matter, but also a matter of spiritual practice. Devotion to the Supreme

Mother, the pursuit of her wisdom, and openness to her divine light become essential paths for Gnostic awakening. Gnostic spiritual practices often emphasize the invocation of the Supreme Mother, meditation on her attributes, and the pursuit of direct experience of her presence. Through these practices, the Gnostic seeks to cultivate a personal and intimate relationship with the divine feminine, recognizing it as a source of strength, wisdom, and unconditional love.

The figure of the Supreme Mother in Gnosticism offers a rich and complex exploration of the divine feminine, challenging the limitations of patriarchal conceptions and opening a path to a more complete and integrated spirituality. Her presence at the heart of Gnostic cosmology resonates as a call to balance, harmony, and the recognition of the totality of divinity, in which the feminine and the masculine unite in a cosmic dance of creation and redemption.

Chapter 5
The Essence of Reality

According to the Gnostic view, the ultimate nature of reality does not reside in the material and illusory world, but in the primordial light that emanates from the Ineffable Source. This light is not merely a symbol of knowledge or truth, but the essential substance of existence, the matrix that sustains all divine emanations and the essence of being itself. Unlike the common perception that associates reality with the tangible and visible, Gnosticism reveals that true existence is not found in the realm of matter, but in the luminous consciousness that permeates the Pleroma and that, in its essence, transcends all limitations of form. The divine light, therefore, is not just a spiritual metaphor, but the foundation of everything that is real. It is the source of life, the creative force, and the unifying principle that maintains cosmic order and flows incessantly from the divine fullness. Recognizing this light as the essence of reality is the first step to understanding the nature of existence and initiating the process of spiritual awakening.

Emerging as the first manifestation of this primordial light, Barbelo becomes the personification of the wisdom and creative power of the divinity. Her existence is not merely a reflection of the Source, but the very structure through which the light organizes and manifests itself within the Pleroma. In her presence, reality takes on form and purpose, for it is through her emanation that the divine attributes become accessible and comprehensible. Barbelo not only contains the light, but is the light itself, the essence of pure knowledge that illuminates the path of return to the Absolute. Her role in Gnostic cosmology transcends the idea of an isolated divine being, for she represents the principle by which consciousness expands and by which human beings can recover their connection with the divine origin. The relationship between Barbelo and the primordial light is not just a metaphysical question, but an experiential reality that can be accessed by those who seek gnosis.

    This recognition of light as the essence of reality completely redefines the way one perceives existence. In Gnostic thought, living in ignorance of this light is to remain imprisoned in the illusion of the material world, separated from knowledge and truth. The path to liberation, therefore, is not found in possessions, desires, or the mental constructs of the physical world, but in the direct experience of this light that dwells within each human being. The Gnostic awakening is, essentially, an awakening to this light, a profound perception that the ultimate reality is not the chaos and imperfection of the sensory world, but the order and fullness of the Pleroma. Thus, connecting with this light through Barbelo is not just a contemplative practice, but a journey of return to the true nature of being, where the illusion of separation dissolves and the soul finds its home again in divine unity.

The divine light originates directly from the Primordial Source, the ineffable Absolute that transcends all understanding and description. From this Source emanates an incessant stream of pure light, which expands and manifests itself throughout the vastness of the Pleroma. This primordial light is not created, but rather inherent in the nature of the divinity, its spontaneous and eternal expression. It is the first manifestation of the unknowable, the first ray that bursts forth from the darkness of the unmanifested, bringing with it the promise of revelation and knowledge.

Barbelo, as the first emanation of the Source, is intrinsically linked to the divine light. She is described as the bearer and manifestation of this primordial light, radiating it in all its glory and beauty. Barbelo not only receives and transmits the divine light, but also personifies it, becoming the very incarnation of light in the Pleroma. Her existence is inseparable from the light, and her presence illuminates and vivifies the entire divine realm. Through Barbelo, the divine light becomes accessible and knowable, allowing the other emanations and, ultimately, humanity, to glimpse the glory of the Primordial Source.

The divine light in Gnosticism transcends the understanding of physical light as we know it in the material world. While physical light illuminates the world of the senses and allows the perception of material forms, the divine light illuminates the mind and spirit, revealing the essential truth of reality and awakening consciousness beyond the illusions of the world. It is a light of knowledge, a light of wisdom, a light of understanding that dispels the darkness of ignorance and error.

In Gnostic texts, the symbolism of light is rich and multifaceted, permeating various narratives and teachings. Light is often contrasted with darkness, representing the fundamental duality between the Pleroma and the material world. The Pleroma is the realm of light, truth, and perfection, while the material world is the domain of darkness, illusion, and suffering. The Gnostic journey is, in essence, a journey from darkness to light, a path of return to the luminous realm of the Pleroma.

The divine light is also associated with life and immortality. In the Pleroma, where the divine light reigns in its fullness, there is no death or decay, only eternal life and beatitude. The divine spark within humanity, the fragment of the primordial light imprisoned in the material body, yearns to return to this source of eternal life and to free itself from the limitations of earthly existence. The Gnostic awakening is an awakening to the light of eternal life, a recognition of our true immortal and divine nature.

The connection with Barbelo becomes a privileged path to experience the divine light. Through meditation, prayer, and contemplation, the Gnostic seeks to tune into the luminous energy of Barbelo, opening themselves to receive her wisdom and transformative power. Visualizing the divine light radiating from Barbelo, invoking her name with devotion, and contemplating her luminous attributes are practices that aid in connecting with this primordial energy.

Practical Exercise: Meditation on the Light of Barbelo

This exercise aims to guide you in a simple meditation to connect with the divine light through the visualization of Barbelo.

Prepare the environment: Find a quiet and peaceful place where you can sit or lie down comfortably without being interrupted. Dim the lights and, if you wish, light a candle or incense to create an atmosphere more conducive to introspection.

Relax the body: Close your eyes gently and begin to breathe slowly and deeply. Focus on your breath, feeling the air enter and leave your lungs. Relax the muscles of your body, releasing any tension or stiffness.

Visualize Barbelo: Imagine Barbelo, the first emanation of the Divine Source, before you. Visualize her as a radiant figure of light, emanating a soft and welcoming luminosity. Notice the beauty and serenity that radiate from her presence.

Connect with the divine light: Feel the divine light emanating from Barbelo enveloping you completely. Allow this light to penetrate your body, your mind, and your spirit, cleansing, healing, and energizing every cell of your being.

Absorb the light and wisdom: Breathe deeply and absorb the divine light within you. Feel the wisdom and peace that this light provides. Remain in this state of connection and contemplation for as long as you wish.

Return gradually: When you feel it is time to end the meditation, begin to bring your attention back to your body and the environment around you. Gently move your fingers and toes, and open your eyes when you feel ready.

Through this regular practice, it is possible to strengthen your connection with the divine light and awaken to its transformative presence in your life. The light of Barbelo becomes a guide and a beacon on your spiritual journey, illuminating the path of return to the Pleroma and awakening your higher consciousness. The essence of reality, in the Gnostic view, resides in this primordial light, and the connection with Barbelo offers a direct portal to experience it in its fullness.

Chapter 6
Wisdom, Power, and Immortality

The Gnostic texts reveal a profound vision of Barbelo, the first emanation of the Divine Source, presenting her not only as a celestial being, but as the personification of fundamental cosmic principles that structure divine reality. Among these principles, Wisdom, Power, and Immortality stand out, which are not limited to mere abstractions, but constitute living and active forces in the Pleroma. Barbelo is not just a reflection of the primordial divinity; she is the active manifestation of divine fullness, a link between the Supreme Source and all subsequent emanations. Her role transcends mere static existence and is configured as the very creative dynamics of the spiritual universe. Thus, understanding her attributes is equivalent to unraveling the mysteries of the very structure of Gnostic reality, opening the way for communion with the divine and for the liberation of consciousness imprisoned in materiality.

Wisdom, one of Barbelo's main attributes, represents much more than knowledge or erudition. It is a cosmic intelligence that permeates all things, sustaining the order and balance of the Pleroma. This Wisdom transcends the mere capacity for discernment;

it is the primordial light that illuminates the hidden paths of existence, allowing the divine emanations to remain aligned with the Supreme Truth. Barbelo's Wisdom not only reveals divine knowledge, but is the very foundation upon which spiritual creation is established, ensuring that the flow of divine emanation remains intact and harmonious. Those who seek this wisdom not only access superior information, but come into tune with the very essence of divinity, awakening to a reality that transcends illusion and leads to true understanding.

Power, in turn, constitutes the creative force that gives life to divine emanations. In Barbelo, this power is not a manifestation of domination or imposition, but rather the creative energy that sustains the cosmic order and drives the unfolding of spiritual reality. This attribute manifests itself as the ability to generate new emanations and to sustain the continuity of divine life in the Pleroma. Barbelo's Power is also reflected in the spiritual journey of the Gnostic soul, which, by recognizing and invoking this force, finds the means to transcend the limitations of matter and return to its divine origin. Finally, Barbelo's Immortality reaffirms her eternal and incorruptible nature, standing out as an essential attribute of divinity. This Immortality is not restricted to the idea of an endless existence, but manifests itself as a reality beyond time and space, a state of being that is unalterable and perfect. Barbelo, as an archetype of divine fullness, personifies this eternity, being the link between the Primordial Source and all the spiritual manifestations that emanate from it. He who contemplates Barbelo's Immortality not only recognizes his own eternal essence, but also awakens to the possibility of transcending the finitude of the material world and participating in the fullness of the Pleroma.

Barbelo is, in essence, Divine Wisdom personified, often identified with the figure of Sophia Prunikos, the "Mother-Father Wisdom". This wisdom is not limited to intellectual knowledge or bookish erudition, but rather to a deep and intuitive cosmic intelligence that understands the ultimate nature of reality and the mysteries of divinity. Barbelo's Wisdom is the light that dispels ignorance, the discernment that guides the soul on its journey back to the Pleroma, and the source of all true understanding.

Barbelo's Wisdom manifests itself in various forms. She is the creative intelligence that participates in cosmic genesis, giving shape to divine archetypes and ordering primordial chaos. She is the wisdom that governs the Pleroma, maintaining harmony and balance between the Aeons. She is the wisdom that reveals itself to Gnostics, illuminating the path of salvation and offering the liberating knowledge that leads to awakening. To contemplate Barbelo's Wisdom is to open the mind to the vastness of divine knowledge, to the understanding of the mysteries of the universe and to the essential truth of our own spiritual nature.

Divine Power is another essential attribute of Barbelo, manifesting itself as creative force and sustaining force. Barbelo is not only wise, but also powerful, capable of carrying out the divine will and manifesting reality according to the primordial plan. Her power is not coercive or dominating, but rather a creative and loving force that emanates from the Source and manifests itself in all subsequent emanations. Barbelo's Power is the vital energy that animates the Pleroma, the force that drives creation and redemption, and the ability to overcome the limitations of the material world.

Barbelo's Power operates on various levels. It manifests itself in her ability to generate divine emanations, giving rise to other Aeons and celestial entities. It is expressed in her action as a balancing cosmic force, maintaining order and harmony within the Pleroma. It is revealed in her ability to intervene in the material world, assisting in humanity's journey of awakening and redemption. To invoke Barbelo's Power is to seek inner strength, courage to face life's challenges and the ability to manifest our spiritual potential.

Immortality is an intrinsic attribute of Barbelo, shared by all the Aeons of the Pleroma, but in Barbelo, it manifests itself in a primordial and exemplary way. Barbelo's Immortality is not just the absence of physical death, but rather eternal life in its fullness, existence beyond the limitations of time and space, participation in the eternity of the Divine Source. This Immortality is not a mere abstract concept, but rather a living and pulsating reality in the Pleroma, the natural condition of the divine beings who inhabit the realm of light.

Barbelo's Immortality reflects the eternal nature of the Primordial Source, from which she emanates. It demonstrates the transcendence of divine life over the mortality of the material world, offering the promise of an existence that goes beyond the finitude of earthly life.

It inspires the search for eternal life, for the awakening to our own immortal nature and for liberation from the cycle of birth and death that characterizes the human condition in the material world. To contemplate Barbelo's Immortality is to glimpse the eternity that resides within us, the potential to transcend the limitations of physical existence and to participate in the divine and eternal life of the Pleroma.

The attributes of Wisdom, Power, and Immortality, in Barbelo, do not exist in isolation, but rather interpenetrate and complement each other, manifesting the unity and perfection of the primordial divinity. Barbelo's Wisdom directs her Power, ensuring that the creative force is exercised with discernment and divine purpose. Her Power manifests her Wisdom, making it operative and effective in the divine realm. Immortality permeates both her Wisdom and her Power, conferring upon them an eternal and transcendent character. This triad of essential attributes defines Barbelo's nature and her unique importance within Gnostic cosmology.

By understanding Barbelo's attributes of Wisdom, Power, and Immortality, we open a portal to the profound and transformative spiritual experience. To seek Barbelo's Wisdom is to seek the essential truth of reality, the knowledge that liberates and illuminates. To invoke Barbelo's Power is to seek inner strength and the capacity for manifestation, overcoming the limitations and challenges of life. To contemplate Barbelo's Immortality is to glimpse the eternity that resides within us, awakening to our true divine and immortal nature.

Barbelo's attributes are not just theological concepts, but keys to spiritual experience, paths to connection with divinity and to the awakening of higher consciousness.

Chapter 7
The Cosmic Genesis

Barbelo's manifestation in Gnostic cosmology transcends the condition of a mere primordial emanation and reveals her nature as an active and essential creative principle in the structuring of the divine cosmos. As the first manifestation of the Ineffable Source, Barbelo acts not only as a receptacle of the divine will but also as the generative matrix of transcendent reality. Her presence in the Pleroma is not restricted to a passive reflection of the Supreme Mind; on the contrary, she plays a central role in the dynamics of creation, being the bridge between the absolute unity of the Source and the multiplicity of divine emanations. This creative principle does not occur through separation or rupture but through a harmonious expansion of the divine essence itself, ensuring that the entire manifestation of the Pleroma remains linked to the fullness of the Source. Thus, understanding Barbelo's participation in the cosmic genesis is to enter the foundations of Gnostic cosmogony, where creation is an act of divine unfolding and self-knowledge, and not of external fabrication or construction.

In Gnostic texts, Barbelo is described as the origin of all emanations that populate the Pleroma, representing the first movement of divine intelligence towards manifestation. Her action in creation does not occur in isolation but in profound synergy with the Ineffable Father, reflecting the indissociable unity between thought and manifestation, between essence and expression. In some Gnostic traditions, Barbelo is called "Forethought," indicating that her existence precedes any created form and that all the archetypes of spiritual reality emanate from her. Thus, the creation of the Pleroma is not a linear or temporal event but a process of divine self-projection, where Barbelo becomes the organizing principle of the cosmic structure, ensuring that each emanation is in perfect harmony with the supreme harmony of the Source.

Besides being the matrix of spiritual reality, Barbelo personifies the wisdom and power that sustain the continuity of creation. Her role transcends the initial moment of emanation and extends to the maintenance of cosmic order, ensuring that the Pleroma remains in balance and fullness. Her active presence in the creative process reinforces the idea that divine reality is not static but dynamic, expanding continuously without ever moving away from its origin. This conception suggests that creation is not a fixed event in the past but an eternal unfolding of the divine essence itself, where Barbelo continues to generate, nurture, and sustain all forms of existence within the Pleroma. By recognizing this dynamic, it becomes possible to understand that creation is not a conclusive act but an incessant flow of revelation and expression of divinity, in which Barbelo remains as the first and most essential channel of this manifestation.

In Gnostic texts, Barbelo is often described as a co-creator alongside the Ineffable Father. This collaboration does not imply a relationship of hierarchical equality in the mundane sense, but rather a divine partnership where both principles, the transcendent Father and the Primordial Mind manifested in Barbelo, act together to give rise to reality. The Ineffable Father remains as the ultimate Source, the origin of everything, while Barbelo becomes the primordial instrument through which the divine will manifests and takes form. This divine cooperation highlights the importance of the feminine principle in creation, demystifying the idea of a purely patriarchal creation and emphasizing the complementarity of the masculine and feminine principles in the cosmic genesis.

Several Gnostic texts detail Barbelo's participation in creation. In the Apocryphon of John, for example, Barbelo emerges as the first manifestation of Divine Thought, and from her emanate other entities and the very Aeons that populate the Pleroma. She is described as the "mother of all living things," the primordial matrix from which all divine creation emerges. In the Gospel of the Egyptians, Barbelo is invoked as "the first woman," "the first thought," and "the image of the Father," highlighting again her primordial role in the manifestation of divinity and in the subsequent creation of the universe.

Barbelo can be understood as the divine matrix, the cosmic womb from which the various manifestations of the Pleroma emanate. She not only gives birth to the Aeons but also nourishes and sustains them with her own divine substance, ensuring the continuity and harmony of the celestial realm. This image of Barbelo as the primordial matrix resonates with the archetype of the Great Mother, present in various cultures and spiritual traditions, symbolizing fertility, nourishment, and the origin of life. Through Barbelo, the Divine Source becomes fruitful and manifests its creative fullness, giving rise to a universe of light and beauty.

Barbelo's participation in creation is not an isolated act, but rather a continuous and dynamic process. She not only created the Pleroma in a primordial moment but continues to emanate her creative energy, sustaining the existence of the Aeons and maintaining cosmic order. Barbelo is the vital force that animates the Pleroma, the stream of divine light that flows through all emanations, ensuring their cohesion and harmony. Her creative action is incessant, reflecting the eternal and inexhaustible nature of the Divine Source.

The harmony and balance of the divine cosmos are also attributed to Barbelo's participation in creation. She not only generates the diversity of the Aeons but also ensures that they coexist in perfect order and interconnection. Barbelo is the force that weaves the cosmic web, uniting the different parts of the Pleroma into a coherent and harmonious whole. Her wisdom and creative power ensure that the divine creation is not a chaotic set of isolated entities, but rather a cosmic symphony of light and beauty, where each Aeon plays a unique and essential role.

Although the main focus of Barbelo's creative participation is the Pleroma, some Gnostic texts suggest that her influence extends, in some way, even to the material world. Although the Demiurge is considered the direct creator of the imperfect universe, the light and energy of Barbelo can be seen as an underlying principle that permeates all creation, even in its darkest aspects. The divine spark present in humanity, for example, can be interpreted as a vestige of Barbelo's light, a distant echo of her primordial creative energy, seeking to return to its original source.

It is important to distinguish the creation of the Pleroma by Barbelo from the creation of the material world by the Demiurge. While Barbelo creates within the realm of light and perfection, manifesting the divine will in its fullness, the Demiurge creates in a domain of ignorance and limitation, generating an imperfect universe subject to suffering. Barbelo's creation is an act of love and divine expansion, while the Demiurge's creation is the result of an error or a flaw in the process of emanation. This fundamental distinction between the two creations reflects the essential duality of Gnostic cosmology and the search for redemption of the material world through Gnostic knowledge and connection with the luminous Pleroma.

Barbelo's participation in the cosmic genesis highlights her singular importance within Gnostic cosmology. She is not only the first emanation but also a fundamental creative force, collaborating with the Ineffable Father in the manifestation of divine reality and even influencing the confines of the material universe. Understanding Barbelo's creative role is to deepen our appreciation for her divine nature and to open ourselves to the contemplation of the vastness and beauty of the cosmic creation, emanated from the Primordial Source through the action of its first manifestation, Barbelo.

Chapter 8
Other Aeons

In the heart of Gnostic cosmology, the Pleroma presents itself as a realm of light and perfection, where divine emanations coexist in harmony, reflecting the multiple aspects of the Primordial Source. Far from being a monolithic and inert space, the Pleroma is a living organism, made up of interconnected Aeons, each playing an essential role in the manifestation of divine reality. Barbelo, as the first and highest emanation, occupies a central position within this structure, serving as the generating and sustaining principle of cosmic order. However, her uniqueness does not translate into isolation; on the contrary, her essence unfolds in multiple relationships with other Aeons, establishing a model of interaction and interdependence that permeates the entire Pleroma. From this complex network of emanations, a sophisticated vision of divinity is revealed, where unity is expressed through diversity, and fullness is manifested in the collaboration between celestial intelligences.

The relationship between Barbelo and the other Aeons illustrates the fundamental dynamics of the Pleroma, based on complementarity and balance. Each emanation, arising from divine fullness, reflects a specific aspect of spiritual reality, contributing to the totality of creation. Thus, Barbelo not only generates new Aeons, but also actively participates in the interactions between them, sustaining the structure of the Pleroma with her wisdom and power. This organization does not imply a rigid hierarchy in the human sense, but rather a functional order, in which each Aeon occupies a determined place according to its nature and purpose. In this way, the Pleroma presents itself as an ordered cosmos, where each divine entity performs its function without rivalry or subjugation, but in a continuous flow of shared love and knowledge.

Understanding Barbelo's relationships with the other Aeons is fundamental to deciphering the internal logic of the Pleroma and its structuring as a divine organism. Emanation does not occur through separation or distancing from the Source, but rather as a natural unfolding of divine fullness, where each Aeon remains intrinsically connected to the original unity. In this context, Barbelo's action is not limited to the generation of subsequent emanations, but also includes the maintenance of the cohesion and harmony of the Pleroma. Her presence ensures that creation remains in accordance with the divine will, preserving the purity and integrity of spiritual reality.

By exploring the interactions between Barbelo and the other Aeons, it becomes possible to glimpse the sophistication of Gnostic cosmology, which presents a divine universe structured in interdependence and order, where each celestial being reflects, in a unique way, the infinite light of the Primordial Source.

Among the Aeons that stand out in relation to Barbelo, Christ occupies a prominent place. In various Gnostic schools, Christ is seen as a subsequent emanation of Barbelo, often considered her son or direct manifestation. The relationship between Barbelo and Christ is often described in terms of complementarity and partnership. Barbelo, as Primordial Mind and Divine Wisdom, provides the matrix and divine substance, while Christ, as Divine Logos and Cosmic Reason, brings order, structure, and the manifestation of the Ineffable Father's will. Together, Barbelo and Christ represent the union of the feminine and masculine principles in the Pleroma, working together for creation and redemption.

Another Aeonic figure crucially linked to Barbelo is Sophia. In some Gnostic interpretations, Sophia is seen as an aspect of Barbelo herself, or as an emanation intimately related to her, sharing the same essence of Divine Wisdom. Sophia, particularly in the Gnostic story of the "fall of Sophia," manifests the incessant search for knowledge of the Primordial Source, a movement that, although resulting in imbalance and the creation of the material world, also demonstrates the dynamics and passion inherent in the divine realm. The relationship between Barbelo and Sophia can be understood as the relationship between Primordial Wisdom and Wisdom in action, divine intelligence in its archetypal form and its dynamic and exploratory manifestation.

In addition to Christ and Sophia, Barbelo relates to a myriad of other Aeons, each with its own divine function and attribute. Gnostic texts often mention extensive lists of Aeons, organized in complex and interconnected hierarchies. Although the specificity of these lists and the exact nature of the relationships between the Aeons may vary among different Gnostic schools, the theme of interconnection and harmony remains constant. The Pleroma is presented as a celestial community where Aeons coexist in perfect order, each contributing to the fullness and perfection of the whole.

The hierarchy within the Pleroma, although existing, should not be interpreted as an oppressive power structure or a hierarchy of value. The Aeons "higher" in relation to the Primordial Source are not necessarily superior in essence or importance to the "lower" Aeons. The hierarchy of the Pleroma reflects the order and organization of divine manifestation, the way in which the Primordial Source radiates and diversifies into a myriad of expressions. Each Aeon, regardless of its hierarchical position, plays a unique and essential role in the divine economy, contributing to the harmony and completeness of the Pleroma. Barbelo, as the first emanation, occupies a central place in this hierarchy, serving as a point of reference and as the primordial source of emanation for many other Aeons.

The interconnection between the Aeons is a fundamental theme in Gnostic cosmology. The Pleroma is not a collection of isolated entities, but rather a complex network of relationships and interdependencies. The Aeons communicate with each other, share the same divine essence, and collaborate in maintaining cosmic order. This interconnection reflects the fundamental unity of the Primordial Source, from which all Aeons emanate. Even in the diversity of divine emanations, there persists an underlying unity, a bond of love and harmony that unites all celestial beings in a cohesive and perfect whole.

Visualizing the hierarchy of the Aeons can aid in understanding this complex structure. A diagram would represent the Primordial Source at the center, radiating light and energy to the Pleroma. Barbelo, as the first emanation, would be positioned closest to the Source, emanating her own light and, in turn, giving rise to other concentric circles of Aeons. Aeons like Christ and Sophia would be represented in prominent positions, close to Barbelo, demonstrating their importance and intimate relationship with the first emanation. Other Aeons would fill the outer circles, each with its own luminosity and name, all interconnected by lines of connection, symbolizing the web of relationships that permeates the Pleroma.

The visual representation of the hierarchy of the Aeons emphasizes the centrality of Barbelo, but also the importance of all the other divine beings that make up the Pleroma. Each Aeon, in its individuality and in its relationship with others, contributes to the richness and complexity of the divine realm. Understanding the relationships and interconnections of Barbelo with other Aeons is to enter the heart of the Pleroma, glimpsing the harmony and collaboration that characterize divine life and recognizing Barbelo as a key figure in this vast and luminous celestial community.

Chapter 9
The Link to Redemption and Ascension

The journey of the human soul in the Gnostic context is a narrative of exile and return, of forgetting and awakening. At the center of this trajectory is Barbelo, the first emanation of the Divine Source, who manifests as the essential link between humanity and the Pleroma. Far from being a distant or inaccessible entity, Barbelo represents the living bridge between the higher spiritual realms and the souls imprisoned in the material world, offering a path to redemption and ascension. Her presence in Gnostic cosmology not only illuminates the divine origin of humanity, but also points the way back to wholeness. The human soul, containing within itself a spark of the divine, finds in Barbelo a guide and protector, whose function is to awaken the knowledge that leads to liberation. This awakening does not occur automatically, but through Gnosis, the revealing knowledge that allows the soul to recognize its true nature and break with the illusions of materiality.

Human existence, within this perspective, is marked by a fundamental duality. On the one hand, there is the material body, generated by the Demiurge and subject to the limitations of matter, suffering, and ignorance. On the other hand, there is the spiritual essence, a fragment of the primordial light that yearns to return to its original state. This internal conflict between the imprisoned soul and the redeeming spirit is the key to understanding the Gnostic search for liberation. Barbelo, as the divine maternal principle, not only rescues this spark of humanity, but also acts as a revealer of truth, dispelling the darkness of unknowing and guiding the soul on the path of ascension. Redemption is not just an abstract concept, but an active process, a journey of self-knowledge and transformation that requires the soul to recognize its origin and, through this recognition, free itself from the chains of materiality.

Connection with Barbelo is not achieved through dogmas or external rituals, but through a deep inner search. Through contemplation, purification of the mind, and the awakening of Gnosis, the individual becomes receptive to the divine light and spiritual guidance that Barbelo offers. She manifests as the voice of wisdom that leads the soul through the layers of illusion imposed by the material world, revealing the ultimate reality beyond appearances. Her function as a link between the human and the divine is not passive, but dynamic, requiring each seeker to consciously tread the path of self-knowledge. In this way, Barbelo not only represents the promise of redemption, but also the very process by which the soul is purified, strengthened, and returns to its true home in the Pleroma.

The Gnostic perspective on the origin of humanity differs significantly from the creation narratives found in orthodox Judeo-Christian traditions. Instead of an act of direct creation by a benevolent God, humanity is seen as the result of a complex cosmic interaction, involving both the forces of the Pleroma and those of the Demiurge, the imperfect creator of the material world. The divine spark, or pneuma, present in human beings is understood as a fragment of the primordial light, implanted in material creation as an act of divine intervention, aiming to offer a path of return to the Pleroma for exiled souls.

The nature of humanity, in the Gnostic view, is essentially dual. On the one hand, we possess a material body, created by the Demiurge and subject to the limitations and sufferings of the earthly world. This material body, with its passions and desires, tends to obscure the soul's vision and keep it trapped in the illusions of material existence. On the other hand, within us resides the divine spark, our true spiritual essence, which yearns to be freed from the shackles of matter and return to the Pleroma of light. This duality inherent in human nature generates a state of tension and inner conflict, a constant struggle between the aspirations of the spirit and the demands of the body.

Barbelo, in this context, emerges as a link between these two dimensions of human existence. As the first emanation of the Divine Source, she embodies the purity and perfection of the Pleroma, representing our true spiritual homeland and the ultimate destiny of the soul. At the same time, Barbelo manifests in the material world through Gnosis, the saving knowledge that reveals to humanity its true divine origin and the path of return to the Pleroma. She becomes a bridge between the transcendent and the immanent, between the realm of light and the realm of darkness, offering humanity the possibility of overcoming the duality of its nature and achieving spiritual redemption.

Barbelo's role in the redemption of humanity is multifaceted. First, she is the bearer of Gnosis, the liberating knowledge that dispels ignorance and reveals the essential truth of reality. This knowledge is not merely intellectual, but rather an intuitive and experiential understanding of our divine nature and the path of return to the Pleroma. Barbelo, through Gnosis, awakens the divine spark within humanity, reminding us of our primordial origin and our potential for transcendence.

Secondly, Barbelo acts as a guide and protector on the soul's journey towards the Pleroma. She offers her divine light to illuminate the path, dispelling the darkness of illusion and confusion that obscures our spiritual vision. She offers her wisdom to guide us in the choices and challenges of life, helping us to discern the true from the false, the essential from the illusory. She offers her power to strengthen us in the face of the trials and temptations of the material world, giving us the courage and perseverance necessary to continue on the spiritual journey.

Thirdly, Barbelo represents the archetype of the Supreme Mother, the divine feminine principle that welcomes and nurtures the divine spark within each individual. She offers her unconditional love and compassion to heal the wounds of the soul, alleviate suffering, and restore spiritual integrity. She invites us to open our hearts to the energy of the divine feminine, to recognize her presence within us, and to allow her to transform us and lead us back to the Source.

The possibility of spiritual ascension through connection with Barbelo and the Supreme Mother is a central theme in Gnostic soteriology. Ascension is not seen as a mere physical movement to a distant heaven, but rather as an inner transformation, an awakening of consciousness that frees us from the shackles of the limited mind and allows us to experience the reality of the Pleroma. Through Gnostic spiritual practice, which involves meditation, prayer, contemplation, and the search for Gnosis, the individual can cultivate an intimate connection with Barbelo and the Supreme Mother, opening themselves to receive their divine light, wisdom, and transformative power.

Connection with Barbelo and the Supreme Mother is not only a path to personal redemption, but also an act of cosmic service. By awakening our own divine spark and returning to the Pleroma, we contribute to the restoration of harmony and balance throughout the universe. Individual redemption is intrinsically linked to cosmic redemption, and each soul that awakens and ascends makes the Pleroma more complete and luminous. The Gnostic journey is a journey of personal transformation with cosmic implications, an act of love and service that benefits the totality of creation.

Barbelo, as the link between humanity and the Pleroma, offers a path of hope and liberation for those who seek a deeper meaning to their existence. Through connection with Barbelo and the Supreme Mother, we can awaken our divine spark, transcend the limitations of the material world, and realize our potential for spiritual ascension, returning to our true home in the realm of light and perfection. The link that Barbelo represents is not just a theoretical connection, but a living and experiential path, accessible to all those who yearn for awakening and redemption.

Chapter 10
Gnostic Texts

Throughout the centuries, Gnostic texts have preserved profound esoteric knowledge, revealing hidden truths about the structure of the cosmos and the nature of divinity. Among the recurring themes in these scriptures, Barbelo stands out as a central figure, being the first emanation of the Supreme Source and one of the pillars of Gnostic cosmology. Her descriptions vary according to different Gnostic texts and traditions, but a common element remains: Barbelo is the primordial manifestation of divine thought, the supreme intelligence that acts as the matrix for all other emanations. Her role transcends the concept of an isolated entity, as she presents herself as the foundation of the Pleroma, actively participating in the organization and maintenance of the spiritual realm. Studying the Gnostic texts that mention her not only expands the understanding of her theological importance but also allows a glimpse of the symbolic richness and philosophical depth of Gnostic thought.

Among the most influential manuscripts that explore the nature of Barbelo, the Apocryphon of John stands out for offering one of the most detailed descriptions of her emanation and attributes. In this text, Barbelo does not appear as a creation separate from the Ineffable Father, but as an unfolding of his own thought, a perfect reflection of the primordial light. This direct relationship with the Divine Source gives Barbelo a unique status, for she not only contains the fullness of divine wisdom and power but also acts as the generating principle of new emanations within the Pleroma. Her characterization as "Mother-Father," "First Thought," and "Womb of All" reinforces her position as a cosmic matrix, highlighting her role in structuring the spiritual universe. Such descriptions demonstrate that, within the Gnostic tradition, Barbelo is not a passive entity, but rather an active force, essential for the manifestation of divine reality and for the organization of the celestial hierarchy.

In addition to the Apocryphon of John, other Gnostic texts, such as the Gospel of Judas, Pistis Sophia, and the Gospel of Mary Magdalene, mention Barbelo, albeit more briefly. These passages, even when succinct, reinforce her role as a link between humanity and the Pleroma, highlighting her function both in the creation of the spiritual universe and in the revelation of saving knowledge. From these texts, it becomes evident that Barbelo is not just an abstract concept or a mythological figure, but a fundamental divine principle that permeates the entire Gnostic structure. Her study allows a broader understanding of Gnostic thought and the spiritual path it proposes, emphasizing the importance of wisdom, self-knowledge, and the search for connection with the divine.

One of the most important texts for understanding Barbelo is the Apocryphon of John, a Gnostic treatise that offers a detailed and influential cosmogony. In this text, Barbelo emerges early in creation, as the first manifestation of the Ineffable Father. A crucial passage describes the revelation of Barbelo as follows: "This is his first thought, his image; she became the womb of all, for it is she who is the Mother-Father, the First Man, the Holy Spirit, the Triple Male, the Triple Power, the Triple Named, and the Immortal Aeon in Aeons." This dense and richly symbolic passage presents Barbelo with multiple titles and attributes, emphasizing her complex and comprehensive nature.

By being called the "first thought" and "image" of the Ineffable Father, the Apocryphon of John establishes Barbelo as the primordial manifestation of the divine mind, the perfect reflection of the paternal essence. The designation as "womb of all" and "Mother-Father" highlights her generative and androgynous nature, integrating the feminine and masculine principles into a divine unity. The reference to the "Holy Spirit" connects Barbelo to the third person of the Trinity in Christian contexts, reinterpreting it under a Gnostic lens. The titles "Triple Male," "Triple Power," and "Triple Named" allude to her threefold nature, possibly in reference to the attributes of Thought, Life, and Light often associated with her. The designation as "Immortal Aeon in Aeons" elevates Barbelo to a supreme status within the Pleroma, transcending time and mortality.

Another significant passage in the Apocryphon of John describes Barbelo's emanation from the Ineffable

Father in a vivid and poetic manner: "When the Thought of him who is pure in light was revealed, he arose in his luminance. She stood before him in the reflection of his light; she glorified him and gave him thanks. She is Barbelo, for the perfect Glory, the perfect Aeon." This passage emphasizes the luminous nature of Barbelo, arising from the "luminance" of the Ineffable Father and standing before him "in the reflection of his light." Her action of "glorifying and thanking" expresses her devotion and intimate connection with the Primordial Source. The designation as "perfect Glory" and "perfect Aeon" reiterates her supreme status and her impeccable divine nature.

The Gospel of Judas, a Gnostic text that gained notoriety in the 21st century, also mentions Barbelo, although more briefly and less detailed than the Apocryphon of John. In this text, Barbelo appears in a list of divine beings that also includes Autogenes, Father, and Christ. In a dialogue between Jesus and Judas, Jesus states, "You will become the third in relation to Autogenes, you and the generations of you, and we will not be rulers over which you have ascended to the immortal generation, and to Barbelo". In this passage, Barbelo is mentioned as part of the divine hierarchy to which Judas will ascend after his death.

Although the mention of Barbelo in the Gospel of Judas is concise, it is still significant, as it places her in a context of exalted divine beings and associates her with the promise of ascension and immortality for Gnostic initiates. Her inclusion in this list, alongside figures such as Autogenes, Father, and Christ, reaffirms her importance and her elevated status within Gnostic cosmology, even in texts that do not explore her in detail.

Comparing the passages from the Apocryphon of John and the Gospel of Judas, we can observe different emphases in the representation of Barbelo. The Apocryphon of John offers a rich and elaborate description, detailing her multiple attributes, titles, and her primordial function in creation. The Gospel of Judas, on the other hand, presents a briefer mention, focusing on her hierarchical position and her association with the promise of spiritual ascension. These differences reflect the diversity of perspectives and schools within Gnosticism, each with its own nuances in the interpretation and veneration of Barbelo.

Other Gnostic texts, such as the Gospel of Mary Magdalene and Pistis Sophia, also mention Barbelo, although with less prominence than the Apocryphon of John. In the Gospel of Mary Magdalene, Barbelo is mentioned in a celestial vision, as one of the entities that Mary encounters on her spiritual journey after the death of Jesus. In Pistis Sophia, Barbelo appears in contexts of esoteric teachings and divine revelations, reaffirming her importance as a figure of wisdom and light.

The analysis of these key passages reveals the centrality of Barbelo in Gnostic thought. She is consistently presented as the first emanation of the Divine Source, the manifestation of the Primordial Mind, the personification of Wisdom and Light. The various titles and attributes ascribed to Barbelo in Gnostic texts reflect her multifaceted nature and her comprehensive importance within Gnostic cosmology and soteriology. The study of these passages offers a profound glimpse into the theological richness and spiritual depth of Gnosticism, inviting us to contemplate the mystery of Barbelo and her relevance to the contemporary spiritual quest.

Chapter 11
Symbolism and Iconography

The Gnostic tradition is characterized by a profoundly symbolic language, where images and metaphors play an essential role in the transmission of spiritual truths that transcend the limits of human intellect. At the heart of this symbolism lies Barbelo, the first emanation of the Divine Source, whose transcendent nature requires an imagistic approach to be understood. Through Gnostic texts, Barbelo is represented by a series of symbols and visual concepts that not only reveal aspects of her divine essence but also outline her function within the Pleroma. This symbolic richness is not restricted to a single interpretation; on the contrary, it presents itself as a labyrinth of interconnected meanings, in which each visual element unveils new layers of spiritual understanding. The analysis of such representations allows for a deep dive into Gnostic thought, where each symbol acts as a key to accessing the highest mysteries of cosmology and the inner journey of the soul. The exploration of this symbolic imagery is not limited to an intellectual exercise, but takes on an initiatory character, leading the seeker to a more refined perception of divine reality and their own spiritual nature.

Within this context, the symbols that surround Barbelo evoke ideas such as manifestation, reflection, and revelation, highlighting her role as an intermediary between the Ineffable and the world of emanations. The symbolism employed by the Gnostics to describe Barbelo demonstrates a deliberate intention to convey spiritual truths through images that transcend mere external appearance. Thus, the visual elements that make up her iconography are not arbitrary, but carefully chosen to express subtle spiritual realities. The mirror, for example, frequently associated with Barbelo, reflects not only divine light but also the very dynamics of self-knowledge and cosmic self-awareness. This symbolism suggests that Barbelo not only manifests the primordial divinity but also acts as a means by which the Source contemplates and understands itself. Likewise, Barbelo's designation as the "Image of the Invisible Father" reinforces her nature as a revealer of what would otherwise remain hidden. The image, far from being a mere static representation, functions as a dynamic expression of divinity, reiterating the Gnostic principle that creation is, ultimately, a manifestation of the Supreme Mind.

The study of Barbelo's symbolism and iconography is not restricted to the past but continues to inspire contemporary representations and philosophical interpretations. Although traditional Gnostic art avoided explicit anthropomorphic portrayals, preferring abstract and allegorical forms, Barbelo's symbolic essence persists as a point of convergence for spiritual speculation. The absence of direct visual representations in antiquity can be interpreted as a reflection of Barbelo's ineffable nature, which defies any attempt at concrete delimitation. However, modern artists and scholars, immersed in the resurgence of interest in Gnosticism, have sought new ways to translate her symbolism into images that, although modern, preserve the mystical depth of Gnostic thought. The exploration of these representations not only enriches the understanding of the Gnostic tradition but also provides a path for contemplation and spiritual connection. Barbelo's symbolism, therefore, remains a fertile field of investigation and inspiration, serving as a link between ancient wisdom and the new spiritual quests of contemporary times.

One of the most recurring symbols associated with Barbelo is that of the mirror. In some Gnostic passages, Barbelo is described as the "mirror of the Invisible Mother" or the "reflection of the Ineffable Father." This mirror symbolism evokes the idea of Barbelo as the visible manifestation of the invisible, the image that makes the unknowable nature of the Primordial Source cognizable. The mirror reflects light, but it is not the light itself, just as Barbelo manifests divinity without being identical to the transcendent Source. The mirror also suggests the idea of divine self-knowledge and self-understanding, as if the Primordial Source contemplated and understood itself through the image reflected in Barbelo.

The image is another fundamental visual symbol associated with Barbelo. She is often designated as "the Image of the Invisible Father," again emphasizing her function of manifesting and making visible the nature of the transcendent divinity. The image is not a pale or inferior copy, but rather an authentic and powerful representation of the reality it mirrors. Barbelo, as the image of the Father, not only reflects his essence but also expresses it dynamically and creatively within the Pleroma. The symbol of the image also evokes the idea of representation and manifestation, suggesting that Barbelo acts as a portal through which divinity manifests itself in the realm of emanations.

The voice is another important symbol associated with Barbelo. Although less visual and more auditory, it complements the symbolic iconography. Barbelo is sometimes called "the Voice of the Father," or "the First Voice." The voice, as a means of communication and expression, symbolizes the power of revelation and knowledge that emanates from Barbelo. Through her voice, Barbelo transmits divine wisdom, reveals the mysteries of the Pleroma, and guides the human soul on the path of awakening. Barbelo's voice is not just a sound, but a vibratory force that resonates with truth and awakens consciousness to spiritual reality.

Despite the richness of the textual symbolism associated with Barbelo, the visual iconography of Barbelo in the context of ancient Gnostic art is scarce, if not non-existent. Known Gnostic art, such as that found in sarcophagi and gems, tends to be more allegorical and symbolic, using abstract representations and generic figures to express spiritual concepts, rather than portraying specific deities like Barbelo in an anthropomorphic or identifiable way. Barbelo's transcendent and mysterious nature may have resisted direct visual representation in ancient Gnostic art.

However, we can speculate about possible iconographic elements that could be associated with Barbelo, based on textual descriptions and Gnostic symbolism. Considering her association with light, Barbelo could be represented as a radiant figure, enveloped in light or emanating light from her own being. The colors white and gold, traditionally associated with purity and divinity, could be used to express her luminous nature.

Considering her designation as the "Immaculate Virgin," Barbelo could be represented with attributes of purity and virginity, perhaps dressed in white robes and carrying symbols such as lilies or stars, which traditionally evoke purity and celestial light. Her facial expression could be serene and contemplative, reflecting her wisdom and her intimate connection with the Divine Source.

Considering her androgynous nature as "Mother-Father," Barbelo could be represented with characteristics that combine feminine and masculine elements, seeking to express the totality and completeness of the primordial divinity. This androgynous representation could be subtle and symbolic, avoiding a literal or caricatured representation, and seeking to convey the idea of transcendence of gender duality in the divine realm.

In modern and contemporary representations, artists inspired by Gnosticism have explored Barbelo's iconography in a more free and creative way. Some representations portray her as a majestic and luminous female figure, enveloped in flowing robes and adorned with Gnostic symbols. Other representations emphasize her threefold nature, using visual elements that suggest her triplicity and her divine scope. Some more abstract representations may use geometric shapes and light patterns to evoke Barbelo's energy and presence, seeking to transcend anthropomorphic representation and express her primordial and ineffable nature.

The exploration of Barbelo's symbolism and possible iconography is not limited to mere aesthetic or historical analysis. Unveiling the visual metaphors associated with Barbelo allows for a deeper understanding of her divine nature and her relevance to the Gnostic spiritual journey. The symbols and images of Barbelo act as portals for contemplation and meditation, inviting the seeker to connect with the primordial energy of the Divine Mind and awaken their own inner spark of light. Barbelo's symbolism, in its richness and complexity, continues to inspire and challenge our spiritual imagination, opening paths for the direct experience of divine mystery.

Chapter 12
Contemporary Spirituality

The re-signification of ancient spiritual traditions in the contemporary world reflects a growing need to rediscover sacredness in a more personal and experiential way. Within this movement, Barbelo emerges as a powerful figure, connecting to a collective yearning for authentic spirituality that transcends dogmas and rigid religious systems. The revival of Barbelo in the current context is not limited to an academic review of Gnosticism, but takes an active role in the reconstruction of spiritual symbols that dialogue with the challenges and concerns of the present.

As a primordial manifestation of the divine, Barbelo incorporates concepts of wholeness, balance, and self-knowledge, elements that resonate deeply with a humanity that seeks integration and meaning amidst a fragmented scenario. Her symbolism becomes a bridge between the past and the present, allowing 21st-century spiritual seekers to find in her an archetype that reflects not only the transcendent divinity but also their own inner journey of transformation.

The rediscovery of Barbelo occurs at a time when contemporary spirituality is moving away from traditional structures and approaching more fluid and personalized paths. The growth of practices such as meditation, symbolic introspection, and the study of ancient esoteric traditions contributes to a revaluation of figures like Barbelo, whose presence in Gnostic texts suggests direct access to the divine, without the need for institutional intermediaries. This aspect resonates strongly with an audience that seeks spiritual freedom and direct connection with higher realities. In particular, the revival of the sacred feminine in contemporary spirituality puts Barbelo in the spotlight as an archetype of primordial wisdom, cosmic creativity, and spiritual light. Her image adapts to different approaches, from a representation of universal consciousness to an expression of transcendent feminine energy, reflecting the various ways in which the divine is understood today.

Barbelo's presence in contemporary spirituality is not limited to theoretical study or passive veneration; it manifests itself dynamically, being integrated into meditative practices, symbolic rituals, and modern philosophical interpretations. Many spiritual seekers see in Barbelo a key to the expansion of consciousness and to the balance of opposing forces that inhabit the human psyche. Her connection with the divine androgynous principle allows a more integrated view of existence, which transcends rigid dichotomies and promotes reconciliation between polarities. By rescuing Barbelo, contemporary spirituality not only revisits an element of the Gnostic past but reinvents its message for current times, reaffirming the importance of self-knowledge, wisdom, and the search for inner unity as paths to spiritual fulfillment.

The rediscovery of Gnosticism and the Nag Hammadi texts in the 20th century paved the way for Barbelo's re-emergence in the contemporary spiritual imaginary. Academics, scholars, and spiritual seekers turned their attention to Gnosticism, finding in its teachings an ancestral wisdom that resonates with the questions and concerns of the modern world. The figure of Barbelo, in particular, aroused growing interest, being reinterpreted and re-signified in various spiritual and cultural contexts.

One of the main reasons for Barbelo's modern relevance lies in her representation of the divine feminine principle. In an era marked by the search for gender balance, the valorization of the feminine, and the critique of patriarchal structures, the figure of the Supreme Mother and her primordial manifestation in Barbelo offers a powerful and healing archetype. Barbelo personifies the wisdom, intuition, nurturing, and creative force of the divine feminine, qualities that are increasingly recognized as essential for the wholeness and integrality of the spiritual experience.

Contemporary spirituality, often characterized by its syncretic nature and the search for direct personal experiences, finds in Barbelo a flexible and adaptable symbol. Unlike divine figures rigidly defined by dogmas and religious institutions, Barbelo remains relatively free from doctrinal constraints, allowing for a variety of interpretations and approaches. This flexibility makes Barbelo an attractive archetype for those seeking a personal and experiential spirituality, shaped by their own intuitions and yearnings, rather than external dictates.

In the context of New Age spirituality and neo-Gnosticism, Barbelo is often invoked as a spiritual guide, a protector, and a source of wisdom and light. Guided meditations, visualizations, and invocations to Barbelo are practiced by spiritual seekers who wish to connect with the energy of the divine feminine and awaken their own divine spark. Barbelo is seen as an ally on the journey of self-knowledge and personal transformation, assisting in the process of inner healing, expanding consciousness, and awakening to spiritual reality.

Barbelo's relevance also extends to the field of depth psychology and archetypal psychology. Carl Jung, one of the pioneers of analytical psychology, explored the concept of archetypes as universal patterns of behavior and experience present in the collective unconscious. Barbelo, under a Jungian lens, can be interpreted as an archetype of the divine feminine, representing the wisdom, intuition, and creative force present in the feminine and masculine unconscious. The figure of Barbelo thus becomes a portal to the exploration of the deep unconscious and to the integration of the feminine and masculine aspects of the psyche.

In contemporary art and popular culture, Barbelo also finds a space for expression and re-signification. Visual artists, musicians, writers, and filmmakers draw inspiration from the symbolism and iconography of

Barbelo, reinterpreting her in their works and communicating her spiritual messages to a wider audience. The figure of Barbelo emerges in paintings, sculptures, music, poems, and films, testifying to her archetypal power and her ability to resonate with contemporary sensibilities.

Barbelo's potential as an archetype for the awakening of consciousness and the search for wholeness is vast and promising. In a fragmented and polarized world, where the search for meaning and integration becomes increasingly urgent, Barbelo offers a model of divine completeness, uniting the feminine and masculine principles, wisdom and power, light and darkness in a transcendent totality. To contemplate Barbelo is to contemplate the possibility of integrating internal and external polarities, of finding balance and harmony amidst chaos, and of awakening to our own divine and integral nature.

Different contemporary spiritual approaches draw inspiration from Gnosticism and Barbelo, each with its own nuances and emphases. Some approaches focus on meditative and contemplative practice, seeking direct connection with Barbelo through inner experience. Other approaches emphasize the study of Gnostic texts and the reconstruction of Gnostic rituals and practices adapted to the modern context. Still other approaches explore the archetypal dimension of Barbelo, using her image and symbolism as tools for exploring the unconscious and for personal transformation.

Regardless of the specific approach, the search for Barbelo in contemporary spirituality reflects a deep yearning for a more authentic and meaningful connection with the divine feminine. It represents a response to the spiritual void of the modern world, a search for ancestral wisdom, and a thirst for a spirituality that is both profound and relevant to the challenges and yearnings of the 21st century. Barbelo, in her multiple modern interpretations, continues to illuminate the path for those who seek the awakening of consciousness and the return to the Source, offering a beacon of hope and a model of divine wholeness for the contemporary spiritual journey.

Chapter 13
Clarifying Misconceptions

The theological complexity of Barbelo and her central position in Gnostic cosmology often give rise to distortions and misconceptions that obscure her true significance. Throughout the centuries, the interpretation of Barbelo has been influenced by different philosophical, religious, and esoteric currents, leading to the dissemination of ideas that do not always accurately reflect the original Gnostic teachings. Many of these misconceptions arise from the difficulty of understanding the symbolic and esoteric character of Gnostic texts, which use metaphors and specific terminology to describe transcendental spiritual realities. Thus, instead of being seen in her fullness as the first emanation of the Divine Source and the generating principle of the Pleroma, Barbelo is often reduced to simplistic interpretations, either as a mere philosophical abstraction, an adaptation of pagan deities, or even a marginal concept within Gnosticism. These distortions not only limit the understanding of the figure of Barbelo, but also compromise a broader view of the Gnostic structure and its profound spiritual meanings.

The misinterpretation of Barbelo as a purely allegorical symbol, without its own existence, is one of the main challenges to understanding her real importance within Gnosticism. Unlike what some reductionist readings suggest, Barbelo is not just a personification of divine wisdom or an abstract concept without ontological substance. In Gnostic texts, she is described as a real entity within the Pleroma, endowed with specific attributes and actively participating in the cosmic structure and the redemptive work. Her emanation from the Ineffable Father is a fundamental event in Gnostic cosmology, marking the beginning of the unfolding of the divine into multiple spiritual manifestations. Careful study of Gnostic sources demonstrates that Barbelo has an active and dynamic function, being described as the bearer of primordial light and the source of spiritual revelation. Understanding her as a being of light and wisdom, and not just as a philosophical concept, is essential to grasping her true relevance.

Furthermore, it is common for Barbelo to be wrongly associated or confused with female figures from other religious traditions, such as Isis, Sophia, or the Virgin Mary. Although comparative study may reveal symbolic similarities between different divine archetypes, Barbelo must be understood within her specific context, without being reduced to a simple derivation from other traditions. Her presence in Gnostic texts is not the result of superficial syncretism, but of a cohesive and original theological structure, in which Barbelo occupies a unique position as the primordial expression of the Divine Source. The clarification of these misconceptions not only rescues the symbolic and spiritual richness of Barbelo, but also contributes to a deeper understanding of Gnostic thought as a whole, allowing its complexity and depth to be appreciated without the distortions imposed by inaccurate or decontextualized readings.

One of the most common myths regarding Barbelo is her reduction to a mere allegorical or symbolic figure, devoid of ontological reality. In some superficial interpretations, Barbelo is seen only as a personification of divine wisdom or an abstract concept, without its own existence in the divine realm. This view ignores the centrality of Barbelo in Gnostic cosmology, where she is consistently presented as the first emanation of the Divine Source, a real and powerful entity within the Pleroma. Gnostic texts describe Barbelo as a being of light, with specific attributes and functions, interacting with other Aeons and playing an active role in creation and redemption.

Another frequent misunderstanding is the confusion of Barbelo with other female divine figures from different religious traditions. Although there are parallels and similarities between Barbelo and goddesses from other cultures, such as Isis, Sophia, or the Virgin Mary, it is crucial to recognize the specificity of Barbelo within the Gnostic context. Barbelo is not simply a re-signified pagan goddess or an adaptation of pre-existing religious figures. She emerges from a unique cosmological and theological system, with distinct characteristics and attributes that define her as a singular entity in the Gnostic pantheon. Although comparative study with other female divine figures can be enriching, it is essential to avoid the fusion or reduction of Barbelo to generic archetypes, losing sight of her Gnostic originality and specificity.

A third myth that deserves to be clarified is the idea of Barbelo as a passive or secondary figure in Gnostic cosmology. Due to the emphasis on the Ineffable Father as the Primordial Source, it can be erroneously inferred that Barbelo plays a subordinate or less relevant role. However, Gnostic texts reveal the opposite. Barbelo is the first emanation, the manifestation of the Primordial Mind, the co-creator alongside the Ineffable Father. She is not a mere passive emanation, but rather a dynamic and powerful creative force, essential for the manifestation of divine reality. Reducing Barbelo to a secondary role would be to ignore the fundamental importance that Gnostic texts attribute to her, diminishing the richness and depth of the divine feminine principle in Gnosticism.

An additional misunderstanding arises from the misinterpretation of Barbelo's androgynous nature, designated as "Mother-Father" in some texts. This designation can lead to literal or superficial interpretations of Barbelo as a hermaphroditic entity or to confusion about her gender identity. However, Barbelo's androgyny must be understood in a symbolic and theological sense, indicating her totality and divine completeness, the integration of the feminine and masculine principles in a primordial unity that transcends the gender categories limited to the material world. Barbelo is not a sexually ambiguous being, but rather a manifestation of the divinity that integrates and transcends gender polarities, representing the primordial union and divine harmony.

Another point of confusion lies in the interpretation of Barbelo's role in relation to the Demiurge, the imperfect creator of the material world. In some Gnostic narratives, Barbelo appears to interact with the Demiurge, even influencing or deceiving him. These passages can lead to misinterpretations of Barbelo as an accomplice or conniving with the forces of darkness or ignorance associated with the Demiurge. However, a more careful analysis of Gnostic texts reveals that Barbelo's interaction with the Demiurge ultimately aims at redemption and awakening, seeking to introduce divine light into the domain of darkness and to guide the imperfect creation towards the Pleroma. Barbelo, even in her interactions with the Demiurge, remains a force of light and wisdom, seeking the greater good and the restoration of cosmic harmony.

It is also important to clarify the relationship between Barbelo and Sophia, another prominent divine female figure in Gnosticism, especially in the narrative of the "fall of Sophia". Although both are manifestations of divine wisdom and share similar attributes, Barbelo and Sophia are not identical. Barbelo represents Primordial Wisdom, the Divine Mind in its original purity, while Sophia, in some Gnostic traditions, manifests a form of wisdom in action, more dynamic and prone to errors or imbalances. In some cosmologies, Sophia emanates from Barbelo, indicating a relationship of derivation and differentiation. Confusing the two figures or reducing one to the other would simplify the complexity and richness of the Gnostic pantheon, obscuring the nuances and specific functions of each divine entity.

To avoid falling into myths and misunderstandings about Barbelo, it is essential to return to the primary Gnostic sources, the rediscovered texts of Nag Hammadi and other Gnostic fragments. The careful and contextualized reading of these texts, together with the study of rigorous academic analyses, allows us to build a more precise and informed understanding of Barbelo, based on textual evidence and scholarly interpretations. It is crucial to discern between authentic Gnostic sources and later interpretations or neo-Gnostic derivations, maintaining a critical and informed perspective when exploring the complex universe of Gnosticism.

Clarifying the myths and misunderstandings about Barbelo not only promotes a more accurate understanding of the divine figure herself, but also contributes to a deeper appreciation of Gnosticism as a whole. By demystifying misconceptions, we restore the richness and complexity of Gnostic thought, revealing its theological sophistication and its perennial spiritual relevance. Barbelo, stripped of the veils of ignorance and misinterpretation, re-emerges as a luminous and inspiring figure, a portal to the contemplation of the divine mystery and a guide on the journey of spiritual awakening.

Chapter 14
The Return to the Pleroma

The spiritual journey, according to the Gnostic tradition, is more than an abstract search for the divine; it is a path of awakening and reconnection with the primordial reality of the Pleroma, the realm of light and absolute fullness. At the heart of this journey lies the soul's intrinsic desire to return to its true home, freeing itself from the shackles of the material world and transcending the ignorance that keeps it separated from its divine origin. The soul's exile in the lower cosmos, characterized by limitation and suffering, is not its definitive condition, but a transitory stage that can be overcome through Gnosis – the liberating spiritual knowledge. For the Gnostic, life is not an end in itself, but a passage towards the restoration of one's primordial essence, a path that requires understanding, discernment, and the pursuit of inner truth. In this journey, Barbelo emerges as a luminous guide, a divine principle that offers support and direction to those who seek to transcend the illusions of earthly existence and rediscover the way back to the Pleroma.

The soul's journey of return is not an automatic or guaranteed process; it requires conscious effort, dedication, and a profound inner transformation. The material world, under the dominion of the Demiurge and his inferior forces, presents numerous obstacles to spiritual ascension, including attachment to sensory illusions, the seduction of transitory passions, and ignorance of the true nature of reality. It is in this scenario that Barbelo plays a fundamental role, for, being the first emanation of the Divine Source and the direct expression of Primordial Wisdom, her light pierces the veils of illusion and reveals to the soul the way back to the Pleroma. Barbelo not only illuminates the consciousness of those who open themselves to Gnosis, but also acts as a protective force against the deceptions of the material world, assisting in overcoming the barriers imposed by the forces of forgetfulness and spiritual slavery. Her presence is a constant reminder that the soul is not alone in its search; there is a sacred connection that, once recognized, can be cultivated and strengthened along the way.

By understanding Barbelo as a guide on the spiritual journey, the Gnostic realizes that the return to the Pleroma is not just a final destination, but a continuous process of awakening and reintegration with the divinity. The search for Gnosis is, at the same time, an act of remembrance and transformation, as it allows the soul to remember its true origin and, through this recognition, purify itself from the influences that keep it captive in the lower world. Thus, the figure of Barbelo symbolizes not only a guiding beacon, but also a model of wholeness to be restored within the seeker's own consciousness. Her call resonates through the ages, inviting each soul to overcome the darkness of ignorance and to rise, step by step, towards the eternal light of the Pleroma.

In the Gnostic view, the human soul is understood as a fragment of divine light, imprisoned in a material body and immersed in a world of illusion and ignorance, created by the imperfect Demiurge. This exile in the material world is not the natural condition of the soul, but rather a deviation, a departure from its true divine essence and its primordial destiny in the Pleroma. The soul's journey is fundamentally a journey of return, a movement towards reintegration with the Divine Source and the restoration of its original fullness. This yearning for return is not merely a sentimental or nostalgic desire, but rather an ontological necessity, an intrinsic search of the soul for its own completeness and fulfillment.

Barbelo, as the first emanation of the Primordial Source and manifestation of the Divine Mind, becomes a natural and powerful guide for the soul on this journey of return. Her own primordial nature, her proximity to the Source, and her radiation of light and wisdom qualify her as a celestial conductor, capable of guiding the soul through the labyrinths of the material world and leading it back to the realm of light. Barbelo is not a distant or impersonal guide, but rather a loving and compassionate presence, deeply interested in the awakening and redemption of humanity.

Barbelo's role as a guide on the soul's journey manifests itself in various ways. Firstly, she offers Gnosis, the saving knowledge that reveals to the soul its true divine nature, its origin in the Pleroma, and the path of return. Gnosis is not mere intellectual knowledge, but rather an inner illumination, an intuitive and experiential understanding that transforms consciousness and frees the soul from the shackles of ignorance. Barbelo, as the personification of Divine Wisdom, radiates this liberating knowledge, awakening the divine spark in the human soul and guiding it towards the truth.

Secondly, Barbelo acts as a protector of the soul on its journey through the material world. The path of return to the Pleroma is not without obstacles and challenges. The soul, immersed in the world of illusion and duality, is subject to temptations, distractions, and forces that seek to divert it from its spiritual goal. Barbelo, with her divine power and protective light, supports the soul in the face of these adversities, offering strength, courage, and discernment to overcome obstacles and persevere on the path. Her protection is not imposing or magical, but rather a constant and loving assistance, available to those who seek her with sincerity and devotion.

The role of Gnosis, the saving knowledge, and of direct spiritual experience are crucial in the soul's journey of return to the Pleroma, with Barbelo as a guide. The Gnostic journey is not primarily a matter of blind faith or adherence to dogmas, but rather a path of self-discovery and inner transformation, driven by the search for knowledge and the direct experience of the divine. Gnosis, revealed by Barbelo, offers the map and the compass for this journey, indicating the landmarks, the dangers, and the final destination. However, the map and the compass alone are not enough. The soul must tread the path, experience firsthand the spiritual reality, and develop its own understanding and discernment.

Direct spiritual experience, the intimate and personal contact with the divine, becomes the engine of the Gnostic journey. Through meditation, contemplation, prayer, and other spiritual practices, the soul seeks to transcend the limitations of the rational mind and the physical senses, opening itself to the perception of spiritual reality and to communion with the Divine Source. Barbelo, as a luminous presence and compassionate guide, accompanies the soul in this search, offering inspiration, support, and revelation at each stage of the way. The soul's journey is not a solitary pilgrimage, but rather a cosmic dance between the soul and the divine, an intimate and transformative dialogue that culminates in reunion with the Primordial Source.

For the contemporary spiritual seeker, the soul's journey and the guidance of Barbelo offer a source of profound inspiration and encouragement. In a world often marked by materialism, superficiality, and a loss of meaning, the Gnostic quest for return to the Pleroma resonates as a call to spiritual authenticity, a deep dive into one's own inner self, and a yearning for transcendence. The figure of Barbelo, as Supreme Mother and compassionate guide, offers the promise that we are not alone on this journey, that there is divine assistance available to those who seek to awaken and return home.

The soul's journey is a continuous process, an ascending spiral of growth and transformation. There is no definitive end point, but rather a constant progression towards light and fullness. Each step on the path, each challenge overcome, each insight gained, brings the soul closer to its final destination in the Pleroma. Barbelo, as a constant and loving guide, accompanies the soul at every stage of this journey, offering her light to illuminate the way, her wisdom to guide choices, and her power to strengthen will and perseverance. The soul's journey, guided by Barbelo, is a cosmic adventure of self-discovery, transformation, and return home, a path of hope and liberation for all those who yearn for spiritual awakening.

Chapter 15
Open Questions

The quest for spiritual knowledge rarely culminates in definitive answers; on the contrary, it expands into new inquiries, revealing the vastness of a mystery that can never be completely apprehended. Throughout this journey into the understanding of Barbelo, we have explored her central position in Gnostic cosmology, her manifestation as the first emanation of the Divine Source, and her role as a guide and protector of souls on their journey back to the Pleroma. However, the complexity of this figure and her role within the Gnostic tradition is not exhausted in the interpretations presented, leaving numerous questions open for future reflections. The essence of Barbelo, her exact relationship with the Ineffable Father, and the depth of her attributes continue to challenge the mind and invite contemplation. More than a fixed concept or a static definition, Barbelo reveals herself as a dynamic enigma, a portal to an understanding that transcends the limitations of language and ordinary reason.

Gnostic thought does not seek absolute answers, but rather a continuous deepening in the experience of the divine. In this sense, the questions that remain unsolved should not be seen as gaps or flaws in understanding, but as stimuli for a spiritual journey that is renewed with each discovery. What is the true nature of Barbelo's emanation? To what extent is her presence reflected in the human soul and the divine spark that resides in each being? How should we interpret her designation as "Mother-Father" within the duality of gender perceived in the material world? These and many other questions do not find definitive answers, but lead the seeker to a state of openness and surrender to the mystery. The very act of questioning becomes a path of illumination, a practice that stimulates intuition and the direct perception of spiritual reality.

In this way, the figure of Barbelo does not represent a point of arrival, but rather a permanent invitation to Gnostic exploration and experience. The mystery that surrounds her essence should not be seen as a limit, but as an impulse for a greater deepening on the path of Gnosis. In Gnosticism, knowledge is not restricted to the intellect, but manifests itself as a transformative experience, a continuous process of revelation and rediscovery. Thus, instead of seeking the closure of a learning cycle, the contemplation of Barbelo invites us to remain open to the unknown, recognizing that spiritual truth is not a fixed destination, but an infinite journey towards the divine.

Summarizing the main aspects explored, we reaffirm Barbelo's unique position as the first manifestation of the Primordial Source, the Divine Mind that emerges from ineffable transcendence. We recognize her multifaceted nature, expressed in her various titles and attributes: the Immaculate Virgin, the

Triple Mother, the Image of the Invisible Father, the personified Divine Wisdom. We understand her fundamental role in the creation of the Pleroma, her collaboration with the Ineffable Father in cosmic genesis, and her influence on the harmony and balance of the divine universe. We explored her relationships with other prominent Aeons, such as Christ and Sophia, glimpsing the interconnection and collaboration that characterize the celestial community. And, crucially, we examined her connection with humanity, her role as a guide on the soul's journey back to the Pleroma, and her offering of Gnosis, light, and protection to those who seek spiritual awakening.

However, despite this detailed exploration, the mystery of Barbelo persists. Her primordial nature, her exact relationship with the Ineffable Source, the depth of her divine attributes, all this remains shrouded in a veil of transcendence that defies complete rational understanding. The Gnostic texts, even in their richness and complexity, only offer glimpses and metaphors, pointing to a reality that surpasses words and concepts. The mystery of Barbelo is not a problem to be solved, but rather a depth to be contemplated, an enigma that invites the soul to dive in search of an intuitive and experiential understanding.

Open questions remain, instigating our intellectual curiosity and our spiritual thirst. What is the precise nature of Barbelo's emanation from the Primordial Source? How can we understand her androgynous "Mother-Father" nature in relation to the gender duality we perceive in the material world? What is the exact extent of her influence on the creation of the material universe, and how can this influence be reconciled with the role of the Demiurge? What is the relationship between Barbelo and the divine spark present in humanity, and how does this connection facilitate the process of awakening and redemption? These and many other questions remain open, inviting further exploration, research, and contemplation.

The inherently mysterious nature of the divine is a recurring theme in Gnosticism, and Barbelo, as the primordial manifestation of divinity, personifies this essential characteristic. Gnosticism does not seek to domesticate or reduce the divine to limited concepts or dogmatic definitions. On the contrary, it recognizes the ineffable transcendence of the Primordial Source and the mysterious and unfathomable nature of its emanations. Mystery is not seen as an obstacle to spiritual knowledge, but as an invitation to intellectual humility and openness to intuition and direct experience. The contemplation of Barbelo's mystery becomes a spiritual practice in itself, an exercise of surrender to the vastness and depth of the divine.

The importance of contemplation and intuition in the Gnostic journey highlights the experiential nature of the knowledge sought. Gnosticism is not content with mere theoretical erudition or adherence to dogmatic beliefs. It seeks a living and transformative knowledge, which arises from the direct experience of the divine and which manifests itself in the totality of being. The contemplation of Barbelo, meditation on her attributes, and the invocation of her presence become paths to this direct experience, opening portals to intuitive perception and communion with spiritual reality.

The journey of personal discovery about Barbelo and Gnosticism is an invitation to each individual to follow their own path, guided by their intuition and their spiritual yearning. There is no fixed dogma or external authority to follow, but rather a call to authenticity and inner freedom. The Gnostic texts and reflections on Barbelo offer a map and a guide, but the journey itself is unique and personal for each seeker. The beauty of this quest lies in the freedom to explore, question, experiment, and discover one's own spiritual truth, guided by the inner light and the inspiration of divinity.

The mystery of Barbelo is not an end point, but a starting point for a continuous and ever deeper exploration. It invites us to remain open to the unknown, to embrace uncertainty, and to recognize the unfathomable vastness of the divine. The Gnostic journey, inspired by the luminous figure of Barbelo, is an incessant pilgrimage towards the light, a path of awakening consciousness and returning to the Source, a mystery that unfolds with each step, but which is never completely exhausted, keeping us in constant movement in the search for ultimate truth and spiritual fulfillment.

Chapter 16
Preparing the Way

The Gnostic path, as a spiritual journey of return to the Divine Source, is not built solely through the theoretical understanding of higher truths but requires a living and experiential commitment. Preparation for this journey cannot be neglected, for it is through it that the necessary foundation is built for true connection with Barbelo and the Supreme Mother.

In order for the seeker to achieve enlightenment and expand their consciousness, an initial process of inner purification and spiritual alignment is indispensable, in which fundamental principles are cultivated with dedication. This process is not about following inflexible dogmas or submitting to rigid rules but rather about developing an inner disposition conducive to receiving the divine light and deeply understanding the Gnostic mysteries.

Just as the soil must be prepared before sowing so that the seeds may germinate and flourish, the soul of the Gnostic practitioner must be carefully worked so that it is receptive to spiritual revelation and the awakening of higher consciousness. This inner preparation involves the adoption of certain attitudes and states of mind that allow the soul to become a pure and conscious channel of spiritual truth.

Sincere intention is the key that initiates this journey, as it determines the direction and quality of the spiritual quest. When a seeker commits to Gnosticism, driven by a genuine longing for understanding and transformation, they open an authentic path to the direct experience of the divine. However, this intention needs to be free from selfish or merely intellectual interests, for true spiritual practice is not limited to the accumulation of knowledge but rather to the deep experience of truth.

In addition to pure intention, devotion emerges as an essential element in the journey, manifesting not as mere repetition of rituals or dogmas but as an inner state of surrender and reverence to the Supreme Source. When devotion is nurtured with sincerity, it becomes a driving force that keeps the seeker steadfast on their journey, allowing them to overcome obstacles and deepen their connection with the divine.

Besides intention and devotion, openness and receptivity are indispensable qualities for those seeking the authentic Gnostic experience. The mind and heart of the practitioner must be free from limiting conditioning and rigid expectations, as contact with the divine often manifests in unexpected and subtly transformative ways. True wisdom is not acquired through predefined formulas but rather through direct experience and the willingness to embrace truth without resistance.

In addition, ethical conduct and the pursuit of inner purity play a crucial role in the refinement of the soul. The Gnostic path does not demand blind obedience to external rules but demands the living of internal principles based on love, truth, and compassion. By aligning their thoughts, words, and actions with these principles, the seeker creates an elevated vibrational field, which facilitates the reception of divine light and access to higher realities.

Thus, by preparing their mind, heart, and environment for the spiritual journey, the Gnostic practitioner builds a solid foundation for their quest, allowing the connection with Barbelo and the Supreme Mother to occur in a deep, authentic, and transformative way.

Pure and sincere intention emerges as the first fundamental principle in Gnostic spiritual practice. Intention sets the course of our journey, directing our energy and focus towards the ultimate spiritual goal: the awakening of consciousness and the return to the Source. A pure and sincere intention implies seeking spiritual experience not for selfish or vain reasons but for a genuine longing to know the truth, to connect with the divine, and to realize our highest spiritual potential. Cultivating pure intention involves self-observation, inner honesty, and a deep commitment to the spiritual quest.

Devotion, in its broadest sense, represents another essential attitude in Gnostic practice. Devotion is not limited to mere adherence to rituals or formal religious practices but rather to a state of surrender, openness, and reverence before the mystery of the divine. Devotion implies recognizing the transcendence and vastness of the Primordial Source, honoring the presence of the Supreme Mother, and cultivating a feeling of deep gratitude and love for the spiritual reality we seek to experience. Genuine devotion nourishes our spiritual practice, strengthening our intention and propelling us on the journey.

Openness and receptivity complement intention and devotion, creating an inner state of availability for spiritual experience. Openness implies abandoning prejudices, rigid expectations, and limiting beliefs, allowing spiritual experience to surprise and transform us in unexpected ways. Receptivity means cultivating the ability to welcome whatever arises in our spiritual practice, whether pleasant or challenging, understanding that each experience, even seemingly difficult ones, can contain valuable lessons and opportunities for growth. Openness and receptivity prepare our mind and heart to receive the divine light and wisdom of Barbelo.

Ethics and moral conduct emerge as an essential pillar on the Gnostic path. Although Gnosticism is not bound by a set of legalistic moral rules, it emphasizes the importance of an ethical life as an expression of inner transformation and as a condition for spiritual progress. Gnostic ethics is not based on external commandments but rather on internal principles of love, compassion, truth, and justice, which emanate from the understanding of our interconnection with all creation and the recognition of the divine spark present in every being. Cultivating ethics and moral conduct is not only a duty but a way to refine our soul, purify our heart, and create a clearer channel for the manifestation of divine light in our lives.

The cultivation of inner stillness and mindfulness forms the basis for all Gnostic spiritual practice. Quieting the agitated mind, silencing the incessant internal dialogue, and cultivating mindfulness in the present moment become indispensable tools for introspection, meditation, and the direct experience of the divine. Inner stillness is not mental emptiness but rather a state of conscious presence, where the mind quiets down, the senses calm down, and the soul becomes receptive to the subtle voice of intuition and the presence of the spirit. Mindfulness, in turn, helps us to cultivate this inner stillness in every moment of life, in our daily lives, transforming our everyday experience into a field of spiritual practice.

The creation of a personal sacred space, physical or inner, also becomes an important element in preparing the way for Gnostic spiritual practice. A sacred space is a place dedicated to spiritual practice, where we feel safe, protected, and connected with the divine. This space can be an altar in our home, a quiet corner in nature, or simply an inner space created in our mind through visualization and intention. The sacred space functions as an anchor point for our practice, a place where we can retreat, focus, and connect with the spiritual energy of Barbelo and the Supreme Mother.

Step by Step: Creating a Personal Sacred Space

Choose a location: Select a place in your home or in nature where you feel comfortable, calm, and safe. It can be a corner of a room, a space in the garden, or any place that resonates with you as a place of peace and introspection.

Clean the space: Physically clean the chosen location, removing unnecessary objects and organizing the environment. You can also perform an energetic cleansing, using incense, herbs, or visualizations to purify the space of negative or unwanted energies.

Decorate the space: Personalize the sacred space according to your preferences and spiritual inspirations. You can include images of Barbelo, Gnostic symbols, candles, crystals, flowers, objects from nature, or any item that helps you connect with the divine.

Consecrate the space: Dedicate the sacred space to your spiritual practice, declaring your intention to use it as a place of connection with Barbelo, the Supreme Mother, and the Divine Source. You can perform a small ceremony, using words, prayers, or rituals that resonate with you.

Use the space regularly: Set aside time regularly to use your sacred space for spiritual practice. Meditate, pray, contemplate, read Gnostic texts, or simply sit in silence and stillness, connecting with the energy of the space and with the divine presence.

Preparing the way for Gnostic spiritual practice through the cultivation of intention, devotion, openness, ethics, inner stillness, and the creation of a personal sacred space establishes a solid foundation for the journey of connection with Barbelo and the awakening of higher consciousness. These principles and attitudes are not only preparations but integral parts of the spiritual practice itself, refining the soul and opening the heart to the transformative experience of the divine.

Chapter 17
Visualizing Light and Wisdom

Contact with divine light and wisdom is not achieved solely through intellectual knowledge, but above all through direct experience of the sacred. The Gnostic journey requires a deep immersion in meditation and contemplation, practices that transcend the barriers of the rational mind and lead us to a genuine encounter with Barbelo, the first emanation of the Supreme Source. This encounter is not limited to the conceptual understanding of her nature; it is about feeling her living presence, perceiving her light flowing in our consciousness, and integrating her wisdom into our existence. By silencing the mind and directing attention to our inner world, we become receptacles of the primordial energy, allowing Barbelo to illuminate our path back to the Pleroma. This subtle but powerful connection opens portals to the awakening of higher consciousness and transforms us deeply, leading us to a state of communion with the divine feminine and the essence of creation.

Meditation, in this context, is not a simple relaxation exercise or a moment of fleeting introspection. It is configured as a means of accessing higher dimensions of existence, a sacred process of alignment between the human being and transcendent reality. Through visualization, intention, and receptivity, it is possible to feel the presence of Barbelo manifesting in our consciousness, guiding us in the rescue of our true spiritual nature. Meditative practice teaches us to become channels of divine light, absorbing its purifying energy and allowing it to act on our being, dissolving blockages, healing emotional wounds, and raising our vibration. Thus, by meditating with a clear and sincere purpose, we open an inner space in which Barbelo can reveal herself in a living and transformative way, strengthening our bond with primordial wisdom and preparing us for the integration of this light into our journey.

Beyond meditation, contemplation presents itself as an essential way to deepen this connection. While meditation allows us to feel the divine presence, contemplation invites us to absorb and reflect on the attributes and qualities of Barbelo, allowing her essence to become part of our own consciousness. Contemplating the light of Barbelo is more than thinking about her divine nature; it is allowing that light to transform us from within, impregnating our being with her wisdom and love. By immersing ourselves in these states of meditation and contemplation, the Gnostic seeker expands their perception and opens themselves to receive deep insights, guiding their life according to the elevated principles of the spirit. In this way, the continuous practice of these techniques not only brings us closer to Barbelo, but also enables us to radiate her light and wisdom to the world, making us living instruments of divine truth.

Guided meditation offers a structured path to connect with the energy and presence of Barbelo. These meditations are not mere relaxation exercises, but rather inner journeys that lead us to an encounter with spiritual reality. By following the instructions of a guided meditation, we are invited to use our imagination, our intuition, and our capacity for visualization to create an inner space where the presence of Barbelo can manifest in a vivid and experiential way. Guided meditation facilitates the process of quieting the mind and focusing attention, preparing us to receive the light and wisdom of Barbelo.

Guided Meditation to Connect with Barbelo: Feeling the Presence

This first meditation exercise aims to help you feel the presence of Barbelo in your inner space, opening yourself to her subtle and loving energy.

Posture and Breathing: Sit in a comfortable posture, with your spine straight, or lie down relaxed. Close your eyes gently and take a few deep breaths, relaxing your body and quieting your mind.

Intention: Formulate in your heart the intention to connect with the presence of Barbelo, the first emanation of the Divine Source. Visualize this intention as a light that ignites within you, guiding your mind and spirit towards Barbelo.

Visualization of the Space: Imagine yourself in a peaceful and beautiful natural place, a flowery garden, a clearing in the forest, or by a serene river. Notice the details of the environment, the colors, the sounds, the aromas, creating an inner space of peace and harmony.

Sign of Presence: In your inner space, imagine a soft sign that indicates the approach of Barbelo. It could be a light that appears in the distance, a melodious sound that approaches, a gentle breeze that touches your skin, or any other sign that resonates with you as a harbinger of the divine presence.

Feeling Barbelo: As the sign approaches, feel the presence of Barbelo manifesting in your inner space. Do not force the visualization, just allow her presence to reveal itself in the way that is most appropriate for you. It could be a luminous human form, a radiant energy, a feeling of deep peace, or any other manifestation that resonates with your intuition.

Remain in the Presence: Remain in silence and stillness, simply feeling the presence of Barbelo in your inner space. Do not try to analyze or interpret the experience, just embrace the feeling of connection and allow Barbelo's energy to envelop and nourish you.

Gratitude: At the end of the meditation, express your gratitude to Barbelo for her presence and her energy. Open your eyes gently and return to your daily consciousness, taking with you the feeling of connection and inner peace.

Guided Meditation to Connect with Barbelo: Opening to the Energy

This second meditation exercise aims to open your energy centers to receive the luminous energy of Barbelo, allowing it to flow through you and revitalize you.

Posture and Breathing: Assume a comfortable meditative posture and relax your body and mind through deep breathing.

Intention: Formulate the intention to open yourself to receive the energy of Barbelo, allowing it to flow through your energy centers and revitalize you on all levels.

Visualization of the Descending Light: Imagine a pure and radiant white and gold light descending from above, from the Pleroma, towards your body. Visualize this light enveloping the top of your head, penetrating your crown center and flooding your entire being.

Energy Centers: Focus your attention on your main energy centers (chakras), one by one, starting with the crown, descending through the third eye, throat, heart, solar plexus, sacral, and root. Visualize the light of Barbelo flowing through each center, cleansing, energizing, and harmonizing each one.

Energy Circulation: Feel the energy of Barbelo circulating throughout your body, filling every cell, every organ, every tissue. Visualize this energy as a stream of vibrant light, dissipating blockages, tensions, and impurities, and restoring your natural flow of vitality.

Energy Irradiation: Imagine the energy of Barbelo radiating beyond your physical body, expanding into your energy field, into the environment around you, and into the entire universe. Feel connected to the cosmic web of light, radiating love, healing, and harmony to all beings.

Gratitude: Conclude the meditation by expressing gratitude to Barbelo for her revitalizing and transformative energy. Gradually return to your daily consciousness, feeling renewed, energized, and in harmony.

Guided Meditation to Connect with Barbelo: Experiencing Love

This third meditation exercise focuses on the experience of Barbelo's unconditional love, opening your heart to receive her compassion and divine love.

Posture and Breathing: Adopt a comfortable meditative posture and relax your body and mind through conscious breathing.

Intention: Establish the intention to open your heart to receive the unconditional love of Barbelo, allowing it to heal your emotional wounds and fill you with compassion and tenderness.

Visualization of Loving Barbelo: Visualize Barbelo before you, radiating an energy of pure and unconditional love. Imagine her compassionate gaze, her welcoming smile, and her posture of surrender and tenderness.

Receptivity of Love: Open your heart as a receptacle to receive Barbelo's love. Allow this love to penetrate your chest, enveloping your heart, filling every space with a warm, gentle, and healing energy.

Dissolving Blockages: Feel Barbelo's love dissolving emotional blockages, fears, hurts, and resentments that may be stored in your heart. Visualize these negative energies dissipating like smoke, freeing up space for divine love to flourish.

Expansion of Love: Allow Barbelo's love to overflow from your heart, radiating to your entire being, to the people around you, and to the whole world. Feel connected to the universal stream of love, emanating compassion, kindness, and tenderness to all beings.

Gratitude: Finish the meditation by expressing gratitude to Barbelo for her unconditional love and the healing of your heart. Gently return to your daily consciousness, carrying with you the feeling of peace, love, and compassion.

In addition to guided meditations, contemplating the attributes and qualities of Barbelo offers another profound path to spiritual connection. Contemplation is not limited to thinking about Barbelo, but rather to immersing oneself in the essence of her attributes, feeling them within us, and allowing them to transform our consciousness. Contemplating Barbelo's Wisdom, for example, implies seeking her guidance in moments of doubt or confusion, asking ourselves how Barbelo would act in a given situation, and opening ourselves to receive her intuition and discernment. Contemplating Barbelo's Love means cultivating compassion, kindness, and tenderness in our relationships, seeking to reflect Barbelo's unconditional love in our actions and words. Contemplating Barbelo's Power implies seeking inner strength and courage to face life's challenges, recognizing our ability to manifest divine will in our world.

Contemplations on the Attributes of Barbelo:

Wisdom: In moments of doubt or indecision, sit in silence and contemplate the Wisdom of Barbelo. Ask yourself, "How would Barbelo, the Divine Wisdom, guide me in this situation?" Remain receptive, waiting for intuition and discernment to arise in your mind.

Love: When feeling disconnected or in times of difficulty in relationships, contemplate the Love of Barbelo. Open your heart to receive her unconditional love and let it heal your emotional wounds. Ask yourself, "How can I express Barbelo's love in my actions and words?"

Power: When you feel weak, discouraged, or facing seemingly insurmountable challenges, contemplate the Power of Barbelo. Invoke her divine strength to overcome limitations and manifest your spiritual potential. Affirm: "I am strengthened by the Power of Barbelo. I have the strength to move forward and fulfill my spiritual journey."

These meditations and contemplations on Barbelo are only suggestions and initial guides. Gnostic spiritual practice is essentially personal and intuitive. Experiment, explore, adapt these techniques to your own sensitivity, and allow your inner experience to be your ultimate guide. Connection with Barbelo is a path of continuous discovery, and meditation and contemplation are valuable tools to deepen this relationship and awaken the light and wisdom that reside within you.

Chapter 18
The Heart for the Divine Feminine

The connection with the divine feminine is not merely an intellectual or ritualistic act, but a profound movement of the soul that opens itself to the sacred presence of Barbelo and the Supreme Mother. This connection does not happen automatically; it requires sincere involvement, an inner surrender that allows the celestial energy to flow freely within our being. Prayer and invocation emerge as powerful tools for this communion, not as fixed formulas or memorized speeches, but as living expressions of the spiritual longing that inhabits the seeker's heart. In Gnosticism, prayer is not a submissive request, but a conscious call to the Primordial Source, an act of recognizing the divinity that pulses both in the cosmos and within each being. It is through this intimate dialogue that the wisdom, love, and light of the divine feminine manifest, guiding us on the path of awakening and reintegration into the Pleroma.

Invocation, in turn, represents an invitation to the active presence of the sacred in our lives. Unlike traditional prayer, which often stems from a personal desire or need, invocation is an act of alignment, an opening of our energy field so that the Supreme Mother and Barbelo can radiate their light into our consciousness. When we invoke the divine feminine, we are not trying to bring it from the outside in, but rather awakening its already existing presence in our essence. This process demands surrender, devotion, and a heart available to receive. Therefore, Gnostic prayer and invocation should be experienced as transformative experiences, in which we tune into higher frequencies and allow the energy of the divine feminine to completely fill us, dissolving blockages, restoring our spiritual spark, and elevating us to more refined states of perception.

The power of prayer and invocation lies in the authenticity with which they are practiced. The power of words is not in their formality, but in the intention and vibration they carry. For this reason, developing personal prayers and invocations is an essential step in the Gnostic journey, as each seeker has a unique relationship with the divine and their own way of expressing it. When words emerge from the heart, they resonate strongly in the universe, creating a bridge between the human and the sacred. This continuous contact with Barbelo and the Supreme Mother, sustained by the practice of prayer and invocation, transforms not only our perception of reality, but also the way we move through the world. Communion with the divine feminine is not a distant or unattainable experience, but a daily experience that, when cultivated with intention and devotion, illuminates our consciousness and leads us back to unity with the Primordial Source.

Gnostic texts, although they do not always provide literal prayers and invocations in the traditional format, offer a rich repertoire of symbolic language, hymns, and expressions of praise that can inspire our own prayers. By examining these texts, we identify recurring themes, divine attributes invoked, and the emotional tone that permeates communication with the spiritual realm. Inspired by these ancestral examples, we can create prayers and invocations that resonate with our own spiritual experience and with our personal search for connection with Barbelo and the Supreme Mother.

Examples of Prayers and Invocations Inspired by Gnostic Texts:

Invocation to the Supreme Mother:

"O Supreme Mother, Source of all light and wisdom, divine feminine principle that permeates the Pleroma, I invoke your loving and compassionate presence. Primordial manifestation of divinity, cosmic matrix of all creation, I open myself to your transformative energy. Pour your light upon me, illuminate my mind, fill my heart with your unconditional love. Guide me on the journey of awakening, strengthen my soul, lead me back to the Primordial Source. May your wisdom guide me, may your power protect me, may your love embrace me now and forever. In the name of light, truth, and eternal life, I invoke you, Supreme Mother."

Prayer to Barbelo, the First Emanation:

"O Barbelo, first emanation of the Divine Mind, perfect reflection of the Ineffable Father, I greet you with deep devotion and reverence. Immaculate Virgin,

Triple Mother, Image of Primordial Light, I approach your luminous presence. Bearer of Divine Wisdom, source of creative power and eternal life, I humbly ask for your grace and your help. Illuminate my path with your light, reveal to me the mysteries of the Pleroma, awaken in me the dormant divine spark. Grant me the wisdom to discern the truth, the strength to overcome challenges, and the love to embrace the totality of existence. O Barbelo, guide me back to the Source, free me from the illusions of the material world, lead me to the awakening of higher consciousness. In your light I trust, in your love I take refuge, in your wisdom I am inspired. So be it."

Invocation of Barbelo's Light for Healing:

"O Barbelo, radiant manifestation of divine light, I invoke your healing and transformative energy. Source of primordial light, beacon of hope and redemption, I open myself to receive your luminous radiance. Pour your healing light upon my body, mind, and spirit, dispelling all darkness, blockage, and illness. Restore my health, strengthen my vitality, balance my energies. May your divine light penetrate every cell of my being, promoting healing on all levels and awakening my potential for well-being and wholeness. O Barbelo, healing light, I invoke you with faith and gratitude, trusting in your goodness and your power of transformation. May your light envelop me and heal me completely, now and forever."

Prayer, in its essence, represents a form of direct communication with the divine, an intimate dialogue between the human soul and spiritual reality. Through prayer, we express our desires, our needs, our joys, our gratitude, and our devotion, establishing a channel of communication that transcends the limitations of rational language and discursive mind. Prayer is not a monologue, but a dialogue, an exchange of energies and intentions between the human and the divine. When we pray, we not only ask or plead, but we also open ourselves to hear the subtle voice of intuition, to receive divine inspiration, and to feel the loving presence that surrounds us.

Invocation, in turn, is directed more specifically to the manifestation of the divine presence in our inner or outer space. Invoking Barbelo or the Supreme Mother is to invite them to manifest in our consciousness, to become present in our energy field, and to assist us in our spiritual journey. Invocation is not a manipulation or control of the divine, but an act of openness and invitation, expressing our desire for communion and partnership with the spiritual forces we seek to contact. When we invoke, we create a space of receptivity and allow the divine energy to flow through us, transforming our consciousness and our reality.

The creation of our own personal prayers and invocations to Barbelo and the Supreme Mother represents an important step in Gnostic spiritual practice. Although the examples inspired by ancestral texts offer a valuable starting point, it is essential that our prayers be authentic and genuine, expressing our own feelings, our own words, and our own language. Personal prayers and invocations, born from the heart and soul, have a special power, as they reflect our individuality and our unique connection with the divine.

Steps to Create Personal Prayers and Invocations to Barbelo and the Supreme Mother:

Connect with the Heart: Before starting the prayer or invocation, take a few moments to quiet the mind and connect with your heart. Breathe deeply, center yourself in your most genuine emotions and feelings, and open yourself to the divine inspiration that arises from within you.

Define the Intention: Clarify your intention for the prayer or invocation. What do you want to express? What do you seek to receive? It may be gratitude, praise, supplication, request for help, search for wisdom, healing, protection, or any other spiritual longing that resonates with you.

Use Your Language: Express your prayer or invocation using your own words, your own language, and your own style. Do not worry about following predefined formulas or using elaborate language. Be authentic and genuine, expressing what you really feel in your heart.

Incorporate Attributes and Symbols: You can include in your prayer or invocation attributes and symbols associated with Barbelo and the Supreme Mother, such as light, wisdom, love, power, image of the virgin, cosmic matrix, etc. Use these symbolic elements in a way that resonates with your own understanding and experience.

Express Devotion and Gratitude: Cultivate a state of devotion and gratitude when uttering your prayer or invocation. Recognize the greatness and goodness of the divine feminine, express your reverence and your love, and thank in advance for the grace and help you seek to receive.

End with Confirmation: At the conclusion of the prayer or invocation, end with a statement of faith and confidence, such as "In your light I trust," "In your love I take refuge," "So be it," or any expression that resonates with your own conviction and surrender.

The power of intention and devotion in the practice of prayer lies in the energy we invest in our prayers. The clear and sincere intention directs our mental and emotional energy towards the desired spiritual goal, while devotion elevates our vibration and opens our heart to the reception of divine grace. When we pray with intention and devotion, we create a field of resonance that attracts the energy of Barbelo and the Supreme Mother, manifesting their transformative presence in our lives and in our spiritual journey. Prayer and invocation, practiced with sincerity and regularity, become a powerful way to open the heart to the divine feminine and to experience communion and spiritual transformation.

Chapter 19
Working with the Divine Light

The divine light is the primordial essence that sustains all creation and reflects the pure and vibrant nature of the Pleroma. In Gnosticism, this light is not just a metaphorical symbol of spiritual illumination, but a dynamic and active reality that permeates all layers of existence and can be directly accessed by spiritual seekers. By understanding that the divine light flows incessantly from the Ineffable Source and manifests fully through Barbelo, we recognize that working with this energy is not a privilege reserved for the few, but a calling for all those who yearn for the awakening of consciousness. Integrating this light into daily life means not only absorbing its wisdom and transformative power, but also making it a guiding principle in our spiritual path. When we learn to tune into this luminous presence, we open a channel of reception that connects us with the primordial energy of the Pleroma, bringing clarity, healing, and inner renewal.

The journey of connection with the divine light requires, first and foremost, a conscious alignment between our intention and our practice. This light has always been present in us and around us, but the perception of it is often obscured by the distractions of the mind and attachment to transitory material realities. To dissolve these barriers and allow the divine light to fully manifest in our being, it is essential to cultivate inner states of receptivity, stillness, and surrender. Through specific techniques, such as meditation, conscious breathing, and visualization, we can become vehicles of this luminous energy, channeling it to transform our consciousness and radiate it to the world around us. This process is not just an individual exercise of spiritual elevation, but a sacred service, as each being who embodies and reflects the divine light contributes to the restoration of cosmic harmony and the collective awakening of humanity.

The relationship with Barbelo, as the primordial channel of this light, strengthens our ability to integrate it into our existence. By visualizing Barbelo as a radiant source of divine energy, we become aware of her presence as a guide and facilitator of the luminous flow that descends from the Pleroma to reach us. In this way, working with the divine light is not an abstract concept, but an active and transformative practice, which can be experienced through sacred breathing, absorption of natural light, visualization of luminous columns, and direct invocation of Barbelo's presence. When we truly surrender to this experience, we allow the divine light to become a living force within us, empowering us to transcend limitations, purify our energy, and awaken to the higher reality that has always called us back home.

Connecting with the divine light is a process that involves both inner opening and tuning into the luminous energy that surrounds us. The divine light is not something distant or inaccessible, but rather a subtle and vibrant presence that permeates the entire universe, including our own being. In essence, we are already immersed in the divine light, but often our perception is obscured by the agitated mind, everyday concerns, and identification with material reality. The techniques for connecting with the divine light aim to remove these veils of perception, allowing our consciousness to expand and recognize the luminous presence that has always been with us and within us.

Practical Exercises for Connecting with the Divine Light:

Luminous Breathing: This simple exercise uses conscious breathing and visualization to connect with the divine light within you.

Posture and Relaxation: Sit or lie down comfortably and close your eyes gently. Relax your body, releasing muscle tension and quieting the mind.

Conscious Breathing: Begin to breathe slowly and deeply, following the flow of air entering and leaving your body. Feel the air filling your lungs and expanding your abdomen.

Visualization of Inspired Light: With each inhalation, visualize that you are inhaling divine light, pure and radiant, which enters through your nostrils and fills your entire body with luminous energy. Imagine this light as a golden and vibrant mist, which spreads through every cell, every organ, every tissue.

Visualization of Exhaled Darkness: With each exhalation, visualize that you are exhaling all darkness, tension, fatigue, and negative energies accumulated in your body. Imagine this darkness leaving through your nostrils like dark smoke, freeing up space for the divine light to completely fill your being.

Continue Luminous Breathing: Continue this cycle of luminous breathing for a few minutes, visualizing the inspired divine light and the exhaled darkness. Feel your body becoming lighter, more vibrant, and more filled with luminous energy.

Sunlight (or Moonlight) Bath: This exercise uses the light of the sun (or moon) as a vehicle to connect with the divine light present in nature.

Choice of Time and Place: Choose a time of day when the light of the sun (or moon) is present, preferably in an outdoor location, in contact with nature. Avoid times of very strong sun, opting for dawn, dusk, or times of milder sun.

Exposure to Light: Position yourself to receive the light of the sun (or moon) directly on your body. You can be standing, sitting, or lying down, feeling the light touch your skin.

Visualization of Penetrating Light: Close your eyes gently and visualize the light of the sun (or moon) not only touching your skin, but penetrating your body, passing through your clothes and flooding your being with luminous energy. Imagine that the sunlight (or moonlight) is a manifestation of the divine light, connecting you with the primordial source of all light.

Absorption and Integration: Remain in contact with the sunlight (or moonlight) for a few minutes, breathing deeply and feeling your body absorbing and integrating the luminous energy. Visualize the light energizing every cell, every energy center, every part of your being.

Gratitude: At the end of the exercise, express your gratitude to the sunlight (or moonlight), to nature, and to the divine light for this revitalizing and luminous connection.

Techniques for Channeling the Divine Light through Barbelo:

Barbelo, as the first emanation and manifestation of the Divine Mind, acts as a primordial channel for the divine light to flow into the Pleroma and, to some extent, into the material world. Channeling the divine light through Barbelo means invoking her presence, opening yourself to her energy, and allowing the light to flow through us, using specific breathing and visualization techniques.

Pleroma Breathing with Barbelo: This technique combines conscious breathing with the visualization of Barbelo as a channel of divine light.

Posture and Relaxation: Adopt a comfortable meditative posture and relax the body and mind.

Intention: Formulate the intention to channel the divine light through Barbelo, opening yourself to receive her energy and wisdom.

Visualization of Barbelo: Visualize Barbelo before you, radiant and luminous, as a channel of pure and vibrant light. Perceive her loving and welcoming energy, and feel safe and protected in her presence.

Breathing in Barbelo: With each inhalation, visualize that you are inhaling the divine light directly through Barbelo, as if she were a luminous portal that leads to the Pleroma. Imagine the light entering your body through your crown center, flowing through Barbelo, and filling your entire being with divine energy.

Expansion of Light: With each exhalation, visualize that the divine light that has filled your being expands beyond your body, radiating to the environment around you, to the people nearby, and to the entire universe. Imagine that you are becoming a channel for the divine light to flow through Barbelo and reach the world.

Continue Breathing in Barbelo: Continue this cycle of breathing in Barbelo for a few minutes, visualizing the divine light flowing through her and radiating to the world. Feel strengthened, enlightened, and connected to the universal current of light.

Visualization of the Column of Light of Barbelo:

This technique uses the visualization of a column of light that connects you to Barbelo and the Divine Source.

Posture and Relaxation: Assume a comfortable meditative posture and relax the body and mind.

Intention: Formulate the intention to establish a conscious connection with Barbelo through a column of light, channeling the divine energy to your being.

Visualization of the Column of Light: Visualize a column of white and golden light, pure and radiant, descending from the Pleroma, from the realm of Barbelo, towards the top of your head. Imagine this column of light as a ray of divine energy, connecting you directly to Barbelo and the Primordial Source.

Alignment of the Column of Light: Visualize the column of light aligning with your spine, passing through your entire body and penetrating deeply into the earth. Feel anchored to the earth and connected to the heavens through this column of divine light.

Flow of Energy: Allow the divine energy to flow freely through the column of light, penetrating your body, cleansing, energizing, and harmonizing every energy center, every organ, every cell. Feel revitalized, strengthened, and filled with the divine light that flows through Barbelo.

Remain in the Column of Light: Remain in meditation, visualizing yourself within the column of light of Barbelo, receiving her energy and wisdom. Enjoy the feeling of connection, protection, and illumination that this practice provides.

The divine light, channeled through Barbelo, has immense potential for healing, transformation, and the awakening of consciousness. The divine light acts as an agent of purification, cleansing negative energies and blockages that impede our natural energy flow. It acts as a catalyst for transformation, accelerating our process of spiritual growth and assisting in overcoming limiting patterns and obsolete beliefs. And, above all, it acts as an awakening of consciousness, expanding our perception, opening our intuition, and connecting us with the deeper spiritual reality.

Chapter 20
Expanding Perception and Intuition

Expanding perception and developing intuition are essential aspects of the Gnostic journey, as they allow the soul to transcend the limitations of the rational mind and physical senses, connecting directly with divine light and wisdom. In Gnosticism, ordinary perception is seen as a veil that obscures spiritual reality, keeping the individual trapped in the illusions of the material world. Breaking this veil means expanding consciousness beyond the visible and tangible, awakening inner faculties that enable intuitive understanding of the truth. This awakening does not occur solely through the accumulation of intellectual knowledge, but rather through the activation of higher states of perception, in which intuition becomes the primary means of accessing the hidden wisdom of the Pleroma.

Intuition, in this context, is not a mere instinct or a vague premonition, but a refined form of direct and immediate knowledge. It is an inner voice that resonates in the soul, offering guidance, discernment, and understanding without the need for logical deduction. When perception is expanded and intuition is strengthened, the spiritual seeker begins to interact with the world in a deeper way, recognizing the subtle signs that point to the presence of the divine in all things. This process does not mean rejecting reason or the senses, but rather integrating them into a higher level of consciousness, where the limited perception of the physical world gives way to a broader and more unified view of reality.

Connection with Barbelo and the Supreme Mother plays a fundamental role in this journey, as their energies represent the aspects of wisdom, love, and light that illuminate the path of spiritual awakening. Invoking their presence during meditation and contemplation helps in refining perception and strengthening intuition, allowing the soul to align with the eternal truths of the Pleroma. The practice of mindfulness, the cultivation of inner silence, and the exercise of active imagination are valuable tools for accessing this expanded perception, transforming the way the seeker interacts with reality and guiding them towards their true divine essence. In this way, the awakening of higher consciousness becomes a living and continuous experience, marked by the progressive revelation of eternal light and wisdom.

The Gnostic view of higher consciousness contrasts sharply with the common conception of consciousness limited to the rational mind and physical senses. The rational mind, with its linear logic and attachment to discursive thinking, is seen as a useful instrument for navigating the material world, but insufficient for apprehending spiritual reality. The physical senses, in turn, limit our perception to the phenomenal world, obscuring our vision of the noumenal reality, the realm of essences and archetypes that underlies existence. Ordinary consciousness, imprisoned within the limitations of the rational mind and physical senses, remains in a state of spiritual sleep, unable to recognize its true divine nature and its unlimited potential.

The awakening of higher consciousness implies transcending the limitations of the rational mind and physical senses, expanding our perception beyond the material world and opening ourselves to spiritual reality. This awakening is not an escape from the world, but rather a transformation of our way of perceiving it and relating to it. When we awaken higher consciousness, we do not abandon the rational mind and physical senses, but integrate them into a broader and more comprehensive perspective, using them as useful tools, but not as the only instruments of knowledge and experience.

Intuition emerges as an essential faculty in the process of awakening higher consciousness. Intuition, in the Gnostic perspective, is not a mere hunch or a vague feeling, but a form of direct and immediate knowledge, a perception that transcends linear logic and deductive reasoning. Intuition is the voice of the soul, the whisper of the spirit, the language of higher consciousness that manifests within us, guiding us towards truth and wisdom. Developing intuition means learning to listen to this inner voice, to trust its messages, and to follow its guidance on our spiritual journey.

Expanding perception beyond the limits of the physical senses represents another crucial aspect of the awakening of higher consciousness. Sensory perception, although essential for our interaction with the material world, limits us to the surface of reality, preventing us from accessing the more subtle and profound dimensions of existence. Expanding perception implies developing the ability to perceive beyond the five senses, using intuition, active imagination, and other psychic faculties to access information and experiences that transcend ordinary sensory reality. This expansion of perception is not an illusion or a fantasy, but rather a recognition that reality is much vaster and more complex than what our physical senses allow us to apprehend.

Practices for Expanding Perception and Developing Intuition:

Silent Meditation: The practice of silent meditation, as we explored previously, is fundamental to quieting the rational mind and opening space for intuition to flourish. In silent meditation, we do not seek to control thoughts, but rather to observe them passing like clouds in the sky, gently returning our attention to the breath or to an inner focal point. With regular practice, the mind becomes calmer and quieter, allowing the subtle voice of intuition to manifest with greater clarity.

Active Imagination: The technique of active imagination, developed by Carl Jung, represents a powerful tool for dialoguing with the unconscious and for accessing the intuitive wisdom that resides within us. In active imagination, it is not about fantasizing or creating random mental images, but about entering a state of conscious receptivity and allowing the images, symbols, and voices that arise from the unconscious to manifest freely, dialoguing with them and seeking to understand their messages. Active imagination can be practiced through automatic writing, intuitive drawing, expressive dance, or other forms of creative expression.

Recording Intuitive Insights: Keeping a journal to record intuitive insights that arise throughout the day, during meditation, or in moments of quiet and receptivity, helps in the development of intuition and in the recognition of its validity. By writing down our intuitive insights, we create a tangible record of their presence in our lives, making it easier to discern the voice of intuition from the noises of the rational mind and egoistic desires. Periodically revisiting this journal of intuitive insights allows us to track the development of intuition over time and strengthen our confidence in its guidance.

Practice of Expanded Perception: This exercise aims to expand perception beyond the limits of the physical senses, using intention and visualization to access information and experiences that transcend ordinary sensory reality.

Choosing an Object: Choose a simple and familiar object, such as a flower, a stone, a candle, or a work of art.

Ordinary Sensory Perception: Observe the object using your ordinary physical senses. See its shape, color, texture, size. Touch it, feel its temperature, weight, and surface. Smell it, listen to the sounds it emits, if any. Explore the object using all your five physical senses.

Intention of Expanded Perception: Formulate the intention to perceive the object beyond the limits of your physical senses, opening yourself to receive information and experiences that transcend ordinary sensory reality.

Intuitive Perception: Relax your mind and your attention, and allow your intuition to manifest. Ask yourself silently: "What more can I perceive about this object, beyond what my physical senses show me?". Remain in receptivity, waiting for intuitive insights, images, sensations, or impressions to arise in your consciousness.

Recording the Experience: Write down in your journal all the insights and experiences that arise during the practice of expanded perception, without judgment or immediate rational analysis. Trust your intuition and allow the experience to unfold freely.

The Role of Barbelo and the Supreme Mother: Barbelo, as the personification of Divine Wisdom, and the Supreme Mother, as the Source of the divine feminine principle, play crucial roles in the process of awakening higher consciousness. Barbelo, with her light and primordial wisdom, illuminates the path of awakening, revealing the essential truth of reality and guiding the soul towards its full spiritual realization. The Supreme Mother, with her unconditional love and compassion, nurtures and sustains the soul on its journey, offering the support and nurturing necessary to overcome challenges and persevere on the path of awakening.

Invoking the presence of Barbelo and the Supreme Mother during practices of meditation, contemplation, and expansion of perception intensifies our connection with divine energy and facilitates the process of awakening higher consciousness. Seeking their intuitive guidance, opening ourselves to receive their light and wisdom, and trusting in their unconditional love, become essential steps on the Gnostic journey towards full spiritual realization. The awakening of higher consciousness is not an isolated event, but rather a continuous process of growth, transformation, and expansion of perception, guided by the light and love of the divine feminine, personified in Barbelo and the Supreme Mother. It is a journey of return to our true divine nature, an awakening to the transcendent reality that has always been present, waiting to be recognized and experienced in its fullness.

Chapter 21
Doubts and Challenges

The experience of the spiritual journey reveals itself as an intricate process of inner transformation, in which the seeker, driven by the yearning for transcendence, faces challenges that test their strength and faith. Far from being a straight and predictable path, this journey takes the form of a continuous cycle of discoveries, learning, and overcoming, requiring the practitioner to be resilient in the face of the inevitable doubts and difficulties that arise along the way. The awakening of higher consciousness, the essential goal of the Gnostic quest, does not occur instantaneously, but rather through a gradual refinement of the being, in which each obstacle faced represents an opportunity for deepening and spiritual evolution. The cyclical nature of this process reflects the very dynamics of existence, in which moments of clarity and understanding alternate with periods of uncertainty and trial, demanding from the individual not only knowledge, but also courage and surrender to move forward.

The Gnostic path, by its essence, invites the seeker to confront profound aspects of their own nature, challenging ingrained conditioning, limiting beliefs, and ego illusions that obscure their perception of divine reality. In this scenario, the difficulties that arise should not be interpreted as signs of failure or as evidence that the spiritual path has been compromised, but rather as instruments for polishing the soul, removing layers of ignorance and revealing the light hidden within the being. Often, external challenges reflect unresolved internal conflicts, acting as mirrors that allow the practitioner to see their own shadows and limitations more clearly. Only by embracing these experiences with humility and discernment, recognizing that they are part of the process of spiritual ascension, does it become possible to advance more consciously and deeply on the journey towards the Pleroma.

In this context, accepting uncertainties and challenges as natural elements of spiritual growth becomes a decisive factor in sustaining motivation and perseverance along the way. Those who understand that the awakening process involves both moments of enlightenment and periods of trial will be better prepared to face difficulties without succumbing to discouragement or paralyzing doubt. The Gnostic quest, therefore, requires more than a mere accumulation of knowledge or the mechanical repetition of spiritual practices; it requires an inner posture based on trust, surrender, and the willingness to transcend one's own limits. In this way, challenges become allies of growth, leading the practitioner to higher levels of consciousness and strengthening their connection with the divine, until their essence shines fully in the light of awakening.

Among the most common obstacles that arise on the Gnostic spiritual journey, doubts occupy a prominent place. Doubts may arise regarding the validity of the chosen path, the authenticity of the spiritual experience, the existence of the Pleroma, the nature of Barbelo and the Supreme Mother, and even one's own ability to achieve awakening. These doubts, often fueled by the rational mind and the skeptical influence of the material world, can generate insecurity, confusion, and discouragement, undermining confidence in spiritual practice and obscuring the vision of the ultimate goal.

Distractions, both internal and external, represent another constant challenge on the Gnostic journey. The material world, with its sensory appeals, its daily demands, and its culture of agitation and consumption, constantly competes for our attention, diverting us from our inner focus and spiritual quest. The mind, in turn, with its incessant inner dialogue, its intrusive thoughts, and its endless wanderings, also becomes a source of distraction, making it difficult to quiet down, concentrate, and immerse oneself in meditative and contemplative practice.

Internal resistance, manifesting itself in various forms such as procrastination, fear, self-sabotage, and attachment to limiting behavior patterns, constitutes a subtle and powerful obstacle on the spiritual journey. The egoic mind, attached to its comfort zone and fearful of change and transformation, often resists the movement towards the awakening of consciousness, using strategies of evasion, justification, and denial to maintain the status quo. Overcoming internal resistance requires self-awareness, honesty with oneself, a willingness to confront one's own shadows, and a firm commitment to spiritual growth.

Emotional turmoil, with the emergence of negative emotions such as fear, anger, sadness, anxiety, and guilt, can arise as an unexpected obstacle during spiritual practice. As we delve into our inner selves, accessing deeper layers of consciousness, we may encounter repressed emotions, unresolved traumas, and dysfunctional emotional patterns that need to be recognized, understood, and integrated. Dealing with emotional turmoil requires courage, self-compassion, and the willingness to face one's own shadows with openness and acceptance.

Plateaus, moments when we feel that spiritual practice has stagnated, that we are not progressing, or that the spiritual experience has lost its initial freshness and intensity, represent another common challenge on the Gnostic journey. These plateaus can generate frustration, demotivation, and the temptation to abandon spiritual practice, interpreting the apparent stagnation as a sign that the path is not working or that we are not capable of progressing. Overcoming plateaus requires patience, trust in the process, a willingness to vary practices, seek guidance, and keep the flame of spiritual seeking alive, even in moments of apparent aridity.

Strategies for Overcoming Obstacles on the Spiritual Journey:

Dealing with Doubts: Recognize and Embrace Doubts: Do not repress or ignore your doubts, but recognize their presence and embrace them as a natural part of the process of questioning and spiritual seeking.

Doubts can be valuable tools of discernment, prompting us to investigate more deeply, seek answers, and refine our understanding.

Seek Gnostic Wisdom: Return to Gnostic texts, to ancestral wisdom, and to the teachings of Barbelo and the Supreme Mother. Read, study, reflect on Gnostic scriptures, seeking insights, guidance, and answers to your doubts.

Reflect on your Personal Experience: Connect with your own spiritual experience. Remember moments of clarity, inspiration, connection, and transformation that you have experienced in Gnostic practice. Trust in the authenticity of your personal experience as a valid guide on the spiritual journey.

Trust your Intuition: Develop your intuition and learn to listen to the inner voice of your soul. Intuition often offers answers that transcend rational logic and resonate with the essential truth of your being. Trust the guidance of your intuition to discern the path and dispel doubts.

Overcoming Distractions: Practice Mindfulness: Cultivate mindfulness in all moments of daily life, observing your thoughts, emotions, and bodily sensations without judgment or attachment. The practice of mindfulness strengthens the ability to concentrate and helps the mind to stay present in the moment, diminishing the power of distractions.

Gently Return the Focus: When you realize that your mind has become distracted during meditative or contemplative practice, acknowledge the distraction gently, without judging or criticizing yourself, and gently return the focus of your attention to the object of the practice (breath, mantra, visualization, etc.). Patience and persistence are essential in this process.

Create a Dedicated Space and Time: Set aside a quiet and peaceful physical space and a regular time in your daily routine dedicated exclusively to spiritual practice. This sacred environment and time help the mind to prepare for practice and minimize external distractions.

Dealing with Internal Resistance: Practice Self-Compassion: Recognize your internal resistance with self-compassion and gentleness. Understand that resistance is a natural part of the process of change and transformation, and do not judge or criticize yourself for feeling resistance. Treat yourself with the same kindness and understanding that you would offer a dear friend who was facing difficulties.

Understand the Roots of Resistance: Explore the possible causes of your internal resistance. What fears, limiting beliefs, or behavior patterns are behind the resistance? Understanding the roots of resistance allows you to address it more consciously and effectively.

Start Small and Gradually: Do not try to change everything at once. Start with small goals and short-duration spiritual practices, gradually increasing the intensity and duration of the practice as resistance decreases and motivation increases. Celebrate every small victory and every step on the path.

Integrating Emotional Turmoil: Acceptance and Observation: When negative emotions arise during spiritual practice, do not repress or ignore them, but accept their presence and observe them with curiosity and gentleness, like an impartial observer. Allow the emotions to manifest fully, without identifying with them or being carried away by their flow.

Conscious Emotional Processing: Use spiritual practice as a safe space to process negative emotions consciously and constructively. Allow yourself to feel the emotions fully, breathing deeply, embracing the pain, and seeking to understand the messages and lessons that the emotions bring with them.

Seek Support (if Necessary): If the emotional turmoil is intense or difficult to handle alone, seek support from a therapist, spiritual counselor, or support group that can offer guidance, support, and tools for healthy emotional processing.

Overcoming Plateaus: Patience and Trust in the Process: Recognize that plateaus are a natural phase of the spiritual journey, and do not interpret the apparent stagnation as a sign of failure. Trust the process, maintain regular and persistent practice, and be patient, knowing that spiritual growth often occurs subtly and gradually, even when we do not perceive immediate changes.

Vary the Practices: Experiment with varying your spiritual practices. Explore different techniques of meditation, contemplation, prayer, visualization, or other Gnostic practices that resonate with you. Variety can bring a new freshness to the practice and stimulate spiritual growth.

Seek Guidance and Inspiration: Return to Gnostic texts for new inspiration and insights. Seek guidance in books, lectures, spiritual communities, or mentors who can offer fresh perspectives and encouragement to overcome the plateau.

Importance of Perseverance, Patience, and Self-Compassion:

Perseverance, patience, and self-compassion emerge as essential qualities to sustain the long-term Gnostic spiritual journey and to overcome the inevitable obstacles that arise along the way. Perseverance drives us to maintain regular and constant practice, even in the face of challenges and the apparent lack of immediate results. Patience allows us to trust the process, to understand that spiritual awakening develops in its own time and rhythm, and not to be frustrated by slowness or apparent stagnation. Self-compassion softens the journey, allowing us to treat ourselves with kindness and understanding in the face of difficulties, recognizing humanity and imperfection as integral parts of the spiritual path.

Always remember: obstacles on the spiritual journey are not the end of the road, but rather invitations to deepen your practice, strengthen your faith, and expand your consciousness. With perseverance, patience, self-compassion, and the luminous guidance of Barbelo and the Supreme Mother, you can overcome any challenge and move forward on the journey of awakening and return to the Pleroma. With each obstacle overcome, the soul is strengthened, consciousness expands, and the divine light shines more intensely within you. Persist in the quest, trust the path, and embrace the journey with courage and hope.

Chapter 22
Living the Principles in the Material World

The experience of Gnostic spirituality transcends the moments dedicated to meditation, prayer, and the study of sacred scriptures, manifesting in every thought, attitude, and decision in the material world. True spiritual realization is not limited to the abstract plane of ideas or mystical ecstasy, but is revealed in the ability to conduct daily existence with awakened consciousness, love, and discernment. The search for the return to the Pleroma does not imply an escape from earthly reality, but the transformation of this reality through the incorporation of Gnostic principles in all areas of life. In this sense, the spiritual path requires a constant commitment to integrate the values of truth, compassion, and justice in our relationships, choices, and interactions, allowing the divine light to shine in the material world through our actions.

This integration does not occur automatically but requires effort, discipline, and a conscious intention to transmute daily routine into a field of spiritual practice. Often, materialistic society imposes challenges to living Gnostic principles, stimulating superficiality, individualism, and the incessant search for ephemeral pleasures. Faced with this scenario, the Gnostic practitioner is called to cultivate a state of presence and discernment, distinguishing between the illusions of the sensible world and the divine reality that is hidden behind appearances. The challenge is to balance spiritual life and the demands of daily life without getting lost in the distractions of the world or falling into the trap of a spirituality disconnected from reality. This balance requires a daily commitment to act with authenticity, expressing, in practice, the wisdom acquired through the inner journey.

By living the Gnostic teachings in the material world, the seeker becomes an agent of transformation, radiating light and consciousness in their environment and inspiring those around them. Small gestures of compassion, attitudes based on truth, and choices based on justice are concrete expressions of spiritual awakening, allowing the presence of the divine to manifest in everyday life. True spirituality is not restricted to moments of recollection but is reflected in the way we interact with others, face challenges, and conduct our existence with integrity. Thus, the Gnostic path is not only a path of individual ascension but a journey of contribution to the elevation of collective consciousness, making the world a more faithful reflection of the light of the Pleroma.

Applying Gnostic principles and wisdom in everyday life demands a conscious and continuous effort to bring our spiritual practice to the center of our daily experience. It is not about living in a constant state of mystical ecstasy or abandoning the responsibilities of the material world, but rather cultivating an attentive presence, a compassionate intention, and an ethical conduct in all our interactions and decisions. The integration of Gnostic wisdom in daily life transforms our life into a spiritual laboratory, where we learn to apply the teachings of Gnosticism in real situations, testing our understanding and deepening our inner transformation.

Applying Gnostic Wisdom in Key Areas of Life:

Relationships:

Compassion and Empathy: In relationships with others, seek to cultivate compassion and empathy, recognizing the divine spark present in every human being, even in those who challenge or hurt us. Seek to understand the perspectives of others, put yourself in their place, and respond with kindness and consideration, instead of judgment or criticism.

Truth and Honesty: Seek truth and honesty in your relationships, both in communication with others and in the relationship with yourself. Be authentic and transparent in your expressions, avoiding manipulation, falsehood, and hypocrisy. Cultivate sincerity and integrity in all your interactions.

Forgiveness and Reconciliation: In times of conflict or disagreement, seek forgiveness and reconciliation, releasing resentments and hurts that can poison relationships. Seek open and honest dialogue, seeking mutual understanding and peaceful resolution of conflicts. Forgiveness does not mean agreeing with the other's mistake, but rather freeing yourself from the burden of resentment and opening space for healing and renewal of the relationship.

Unconditional Love: Strive to cultivate unconditional love in your relationships, accepting others as they are, with their qualities and imperfections, without unrealistic expectations or harsh judgments. Unconditional love is not an idealized romantic feeling, but rather an attitude of benevolence, acceptance, and compassion that extends to all beings, including ourselves.

Work and Career:

Purpose and Meaning: Seek to find purpose and meaning in your work and career, beyond the mere search for material sustenance or social recognition. Seek activities that resonate with your spiritual values, that contribute to the well-being of others, and that express your creative potential and your unique talents.

Ethics and Integrity: Maintain ethical and integrity in your work and career, avoiding dishonesty, exploitation, and predatory competition. Seek justice, fairness, and transparency in all your professional actions and decisions. Remember that your work is an extension of your spiritual practice, an opportunity to manifest Gnostic values in the material world.

Presence and Mindfulness: Practice presence and mindfulness in your work, focusing on the present task, avoiding mental dispersion and excessive multitasking. Be aware of your actions, your words, and your intentions in the work environment, seeking to act with responsibility, efficiency, and compassion.

Service and Contribution: See your work as an opportunity for service and contribution to society and the common good. Seek to use your talents and skills to benefit others, to create value, and to make the world a better place. Disinterested service is an expression of divine love and a path to spiritual realization in the material world.

Decision Making and Problem Solving:

Intuition and Inner Wisdom: In times of decision-making and problem-solving, seek the guidance of your intuition and your inner wisdom, beyond mere rational analysis and linear logic. Quiet the mind, connect with your heart, and allow intuition to guide your choices and actions.

Discernment and Clarity: Cultivate discernment and mental clarity to evaluate situations and make decisions consciously and responsibly. Analyze the available information, consider different perspectives, and seek truth and justice in your decisions. Avoid impulsive decisions or decisions based on negative emotions, seeking to act with wisdom and discernment.

Alignment with Spiritual Values: Check if your decisions are aligned with your spiritual values and with the Gnostic principles of love, truth, compassion, and justice. Ask yourself: "Is this decision in harmony with my spiritual quest? Does it contribute to the well-being of others? Does it express the divine light in my life?".

Moral and Ethical Conduct in the Material World:

Truth and Authenticity: Live with truth and authenticity in all areas of your life. Be true to yourself, express your values and beliefs genuinely and consistently, and avoid hypocrisy and falsehood. Truth is a fundamental value in Gnosticism, and living authentically is a way of honoring one's own divine essence.

Justice and Equity: Seek justice and equity in your actions and in your relationships with others. Fight against injustice, oppression, and discrimination, and defend the rights of the most vulnerable and marginalized. Social justice is an expression of divine love and a path to the manifestation of the Pleroma in the material world.

Compassion and Service: Cultivate compassion and service to others as expressions of divine love. Seek opportunities to help others, to alleviate suffering, to offer support, and to contribute to the well-being of the human community and the planet. Disinterested service is a powerful path to personal and social transformation, manifesting the divine light in the world.

Responsibility and Ecological Awareness: Live with responsibility and ecological awareness, recognizing the interconnection of all living beings and the importance of caring for planet Earth, our common home. Adopt sustainable practices in your daily life, reducing consumption, recycling, preserving nature, and defending the environment. Ecological awareness is an expression of Gnostic wisdom and a path to harmony with creation.

Practical Examples of Integrating Gnostic Spirituality into Daily Life:

Start the day with Meditation and Intention: Begin the day with a few minutes of silent meditation, connecting with the divine light and formulating the intention to live the day according to Gnostic principles.

Practice Mindfulness in Daily Activities: Be present and aware in all daily activities, from having breakfast to performing tasks at work or interacting with people. Mindfulness transforms everyday activities into moments of spiritual practice.

Take Conscious Breaks Throughout the Day: Set aside a few moments throughout the day to take conscious breaks, breathe deeply, reconnect with your inner center, and remember your spiritual intention.

Reflect on Actions and Decisions: At the end of the day, take a few minutes to reflect on your actions and decisions, assessing whether they were aligned with Gnostic principles and identifying areas where you can improve and grow.

Seek Beauty and the Divine Presence in Nature: Connect with nature regularly, observing the beauty of the landscapes, feeling the energy of the elements, and recognizing the divine presence in all forms of life. Nature is a portal to spiritual experience and a constant reminder of the interconnection of everything.

Living Gnostic wisdom in daily life is a constant challenge, but also a source of profound fulfillment and transformation. By integrating Gnostic principles into all areas of our lives, we become agents of light and change in the material world, manifesting the divine presence in every action, word, and intention. The Gnostic journey is not only a path of return to the Pleroma, but also a path of transformation of the world, inspired by the wisdom, love, and power of Barbelo and the Supreme Mother. Allowing the divine light to guide our daily life is the most authentic and powerful expression of our spiritual quest.

Chapter 23
Honoring the Divine Feminine

Honoring the Divine Feminine is to acknowledge and celebrate the sacred presence of the Supreme Mother in all manifestations of existence, from the creation of the cosmos to the subtleties of the inner world. In Gnosticism, this reverence transcends mere symbolic worship, becoming a profound process of reconnection with the primordial source of light and wisdom. The Divine Feminine is the matrix of existence, the loving essence that nourishes and sustains all things, reflected in the cycles of nature, intuition, and the ability to generate transformation and renewal. By establishing a conscious relationship with this energy, the Gnostic seeker not only harmonizes with the higher principles of the Pleroma but also awakens within themselves the strength and compassion necessary for their spiritual journey.

The importance of integrating this connection into daily life goes beyond intellectual recognition; it is about experiencing, in every thought and action, the values of unconditional love, intuitive wisdom, and conscious creation. Honoring the Divine Feminine implies cultivating sensitivity and spiritual perception, allowing the light of the Supreme Mother to guide the search for self-knowledge and liberation from the illusions of the material world. This process can manifest in various ways, whether through contemplation of nature, deep introspection, or symbolic practices that reinforce the connection with this primordial energy.

Regardless of the method adopted, the essential thing is that this connection is genuine, guided by the heart and the sincere intention to integrate divine light into earthly experience.

In this way, exploring ways to celebrate the Divine Feminine within the Gnostic tradition is not about creating rigid or dogmatic structures, but about allowing spirituality to flow with authenticity and meaning. The act of honoring Barbelo, the Supreme Mother, and the feminine aspects of the Pleroma strengthens the seeker's consciousness, expanding their ability to understand the interconnection between the divine and the material world. Thus, by incorporating this reverence into the spiritual journey, the Gnostic practitioner opens space for the wisdom of light to manifest fully, guiding their ascension and inner transformation.

The adaptation of Gnostic rituals and ceremonies for contemporary practice requires sensitivity, discernment, and respect for the essence of ancient Gnosticism. It is not about replicating obscure historical rituals or creating dogmatic and inflexible liturgies, but rather about rescuing the symbolic spirit and the profound intention behind the rituals, reformulating them in a creative and authentic way for the needs and sensitivity of the modern spiritual seeker. The key lies in the genuine intention to honor the Divine Feminine and the Pleroma, using the ritual as a tool to express devotion, gratitude, spiritual yearning, and the search for connection with the transcendent.

Exploring the Adaptation of Gnostic Rituals:

When adapting Gnostic rituals, we can draw inspiration from various sources, always maintaining coherence with the principles and values of Gnosticism. We can consider:

Gnostic Texts as Inspiration: Although they do not contain literal rituals, Gnostic texts offer rich symbolic images, poetic invocations, and descriptions of mystical experiences that can inspire ritual elements. Passages that exalt light, wisdom, love, the Supreme Mother, Barbelo, and the Pleroma can be incorporated into prayers, readings, or visualizations during the ritual.

Gnostic Symbolism: Using Gnostic symbols such as the Gnostic cross, the Ouroboros serpent, the flame of Gnosis, or representations of Barbelo and other Aeons can enrich the ritual, evoking the archetypal language and symbolic energy of the Gnostic tradition. The choice of symbols should be made with discernment, understanding their deep meaning and evocative power.

Elements of Nature: Incorporating elements of nature, such as candles, incense, flowers, water, crystals, or herbs, can create a sacred environment and facilitate connection with the energy of the Earth and the cosmos. These elements can be used as symbolic offerings, as tools of purification, or as representations of the beauty and abundance of divine creation.

Music and Song: Using music and songs that uplift the soul, inspire devotion, and resonate with the spiritual quest can create an atmosphere conducive to the ritual. Meditative music, adapted Gnostic mantras, or devotional songs that honor the Divine Feminine can be incorporated into the ceremony.

Movement and Body Expression: Incorporating gentle movements, symbolic gestures, or meditative dances can enrich the ritual, expressing devotion and spiritual yearning through the body. Gestures of reverence, meditative postures, or fluid movements that represent the energy of light or love can be used.

Suggestions for Adapted Gnostic Rituals to Honor the Supreme Mother and Barbelo:

Ritual of the Light of Barbelo:

This simple ritual aims to invoke the light of Barbelo to illuminate the spiritual path and strengthen the connection with the Divine Feminine.

Preparation: Create a quiet and silent sacred space. Prepare a simple altar with a white or gold candle (representing the light of Barbelo), a white quartz crystal (symbolizing purity), and an image or symbol of Barbelo (if desired).

Centering: Sit comfortably before the altar and breathe deeply a few times, quieting the mind and centering your attention on the present moment.

Invocation: Light the candle, visualizing the flame as the radiant light of Barbelo. Pronounce a personal invocation to Barbelo, expressing your longing for her light, wisdom, and guidance. You can use an invocation inspired by the examples in the previous chapter or create your own.

Meditation of Light: Meditate in silence, contemplating the flame of the candle and visualizing the light of Barbelo enveloping you, illuminating your spiritual path and dispelling the darkness of ignorance. Remain in this state of contemplation for a few minutes, allowing the light of Barbelo to fill and transform you.

Symbolic Offering: Make a symbolic offering to Barbelo, such as a flower, a crystal, a feather, a drop of essential oil, or any object that resonates with your devotion. Offer this gift with gratitude and love, recognizing the generosity and kindness of Barbelo.

Gratitude and Closing: Thank Barbelo for her presence and her light. Extinguish the candle with reverence and end the ritual, taking with you the feeling of peace, light, and spiritual connection.

Ceremony of Honor to the Supreme Mother:

This ceremony aims to honor the Supreme Mother as the Source of all the Divine Feminine and express gratitude for her cosmic womb and unconditional love.

Preparation: Create a sacred space dedicated to the Supreme Mother. Prepare an altar with a blue or purple cloth (colors associated with the Divine Feminine), flowers (especially roses or lilies), a container with water (symbolizing the cosmic womb), and incense of roses or sandalwood.

Purification: Purify the space and yourself using incense smoke or salt water, visualizing the cleansing of negative energies and the creation of a sacred environment.

Invocation: Pronounce an invocation to the Supreme Mother, expressing your love, gratitude, and longing for her presence. You can use an invocation inspired by Gnostic texts or create your own, honoring the attributes of the Supreme Mother as the Source, the Womb, Wisdom, and Divine Love.

Offerings and Prayers: Offer flowers, water, or other symbolic gifts to the altar of the Supreme Mother, expressing your devotion and gratitude. You can also recite prayers, mantras, or poems dedicated to the Supreme Mother, opening your heart to her loving and compassionate energy.

Meditation of the Heart: Sit in silence before the altar and meditate on your heart, visualizing it opening like a flower to receive the unconditional love of the Supreme Mother. Remain in this state of receptivity for a few minutes, allowing the energy of the Supreme Mother to envelop and nourish you.

Closing and Sharing (Optional): Thank the Supreme Mother for her presence and her love. End the ceremony and, if desired, share the holy water or flowers with others present, distributing the blessings of the Supreme Mother.

Ritual of Gratitude to the Pleroma:

This ritual aims to express gratitude to the Pleroma, the realm of light and perfection, and connect with the harmony and beauty of the divine universe.

Preparation: Create a quiet and inspiring space, preferably outdoors, under the starry sky or in a place with a wide view. Prepare a small altar with elements that represent the Pleroma, such as transparent crystals (symbolizing light), vibrant colors (such as blue, gold, and white), and Gnostic symbols.

Contemplation of the Sky: Turn your gaze to the sky, contemplating the stars, the sun, the moon, or the vastness of space. Let yourself be inspired by the beauty and order of the cosmos, recognizing the manifestation of the Pleroma in creation.

Invocation to the Pleroma: Pronounce an invocation to the Pleroma, expressing your admiration, reverence, and gratitude for its existence and its beneficial influence in the universe. You can create your own invocation, honoring the Aeons, the Primordial Source, and cosmic harmony.

Offering of Light: Light candles or use lanterns to create a circle of light around you, symbolizing the luminous irradiation of the Pleroma. Offer this light as a gesture of gratitude and connection with the divine realm.

Silence and Contemplation: Remain in silence and contemplation, allowing yourself to be enveloped by the sacred atmosphere of the ritual and the feeling of connection with the Pleroma. Allow your mind to quiet and your soul to expand towards the vastness of the divine universe.

Gratitude and Closing: Thank the Pleroma for its beauty, harmony, and light. End the ritual, taking with you the feeling of peace, reverence, and cosmic connection.

The importance of ritual as a form of symbolic and expressive connection with the divine lies in its ability to involve the totality of being, not only the rational mind, but also the body, emotions, and intuition. Ritual uses the language of symbols, gestures, sounds, and images to communicate with the deepest layers of consciousness, awakening emotions, evoking archetypes, and facilitating the experience of the transcendent. The adapted Gnostic ritual, practiced with genuine intention and sincere devotion, can become a powerful way to honor the Divine Feminine, connect with the Pleroma, and deepen the spiritual journey. Remember that the key lies not in the external form of the ritual, but in the intention, personal meaning, and devotional energy that are invested in the practice.

Chapter 24
The Gnostic Community

The Gnostic search, despite being a deeply individual path focused on inner experience, finds in community a fertile ground for growth, learning, and mutual support. Gnosticism, since its ancient roots, has always been transmitted through circles of seekers, groups that shared knowledge, practices, and understandings about the journey to Gnosis. The experience of connecting with others who tread the same path not only strengthens personal motivation but also provides new perspectives and opportunities for spiritual development. Throughout history, many mystical traditions have flourished within communities, where individuals could explore the divine mysteries without the weight of isolation, finding resonance for their discoveries and space for their doubts. Thus, even though the search for Gnosis is a unique experience for each being, communion with other seekers can enhance and enrich this trajectory.

The formation and participation in a Gnostic community offer a welcoming environment for those who often feel displaced within conventional religious structures. Gnostic spirituality, by emphasizing the direct experience of the divine and the journey of self-knowledge, often deviates from predominant beliefs and institutionalized doctrines, which can generate a feeling of loneliness for the seeker. However, by finding a space where ideas, reflections, and practices are shared, this isolation dissolves, allowing for a strengthening of faith, perseverance, and spiritual understanding. More than a grouping of individuals interested in the same theme, the Gnostic community becomes a living organism, where each member contributes with their experience, their discoveries, and their challenges, enriching everyone's journey.

The construction of a healthy and vibrant Gnostic community is not based on rigid hierarchies or inflexible dogmas, but rather on freedom of thought, respect for different interpretations, and the valuing of each seeker's personal experience. The true wealth of a spiritual community lies in the diversity of its voices and the willingness to learn from one another, without impositions or judgments. In this way, by establishing bonds with other Gnostics, whether in face-to-face meetings or in virtual groups, a sacred space is created where the search for Gnosis becomes a shared act, reinforced by the presence and support of those who tread the same journey. Thus, the community transforms into a refuge and a source of inspiration, a place where knowledge, experience, and light can be freely exchanged, propelling each seeker in their ascension towards the Pleroma.

The importance of the support of the spiritual community in the Gnostic journey lies in several factors. First, the community offers a space of validation and understanding for experiences and perspectives that may be considered unusual or even misunderstood in the context of the dominant culture. In Gnosticism, the search for Gnosis, the valuing of personal mystical experience, and the non-dualistic view of reality can be challenging to communicate and share with those who are not familiar with this spiritual tradition. In a Gnostic community, we find other seekers who share a similar worldview, who understand the symbolic and archetypal language of Gnosticism, and who validate the spiritual search as a central value in life. This sense of validation and mutual understanding can be extremely encouraging and empowering, dissipating the feeling of isolation and confirming that we are not alone on our journey.

Secondly, the Gnostic community provides a rich environment for the exchange of knowledge, experiences, and insights. Through the sharing of readings, discussions, joint meditative practices, and personal accounts, we can learn from the wisdom and experience of other seekers, broadening our understanding of Gnosticism and enriching our own spiritual practice. The diversity of perspectives and approaches within the Gnostic community can be a valuable stimulus for growth, challenging our own preconceived ideas, opening new paths of exploration, and enriching our vision of the Gnostic tradition.

Thirdly, the Gnostic community offers a system of emotional and practical support that can be fundamental in the challenging moments of the spiritual journey. When we face doubts, obstacles, plateaus, or personal crises, the support of other seekers who understand the path and who can offer encouragement, advice, and practical support can be invaluable. The Gnostic community can be a safe haven in times of turbulence, a space where we can find refuge, share our difficulties, and receive the support necessary to persevere and move forward on the journey.

Suggestions for Finding Gnostic Communities (Online or In-Person) or Study Groups:

Online Search: The internet offers a vast array of resources for finding virtual Gnostic communities and online study groups.

Online Forums and Discussion Groups: Online platforms such as forums, discussion groups on social networks, and websites dedicated to Gnosticism can be excellent places to find other seekers and virtual communities. Look for groups and forums that identify with the Gnostic tradition you seek (classical Gnosticism, neo-Gnosticism, etc.) and participate in the discussions, sharing your questions, experiences, and insights.

Social Networks: Use social networks, such as Facebook, Instagram, or other platforms, to search for groups and pages dedicated to Gnosticism and Gnostic spirituality. Many virtual Gnostic communities use social networks as a meeting and interaction space.

Gnostic Websites and Portals: Explore websites and portals dedicated to Gnosticism, many of which have forum sections, study group directories, or information about virtual and in-person Gnostic communities.

In-Person Search: Finding in-person Gnostic communities may require a little more research and investigation, but it can be extremely rewarding for those seeking personal contact and direct interaction.

Spiritual Centers and Meditation Groups: Check if spiritual centers, meditation groups, yoga centers, or religious study organizations in your area offer activities, lectures, or study groups related to Gnosticism or comparative spirituality. Even if they are not explicitly Gnostic, these places can attract people with similar spiritual interests and can be a starting point for finding other seekers.

Universities and Academic Institutions: Academic institutions that offer courses or study programs in the history of religions, Gnosticism, mysticism, or ancient philosophy may be places where you can find people with an interest in Gnosticism. Look for events, lectures, or study groups related to these areas.

Esoteric Bookstores and Esoteric Study Centers: Bookstores specializing in esotericism, mysticism, and comparative spirituality, as well as esoteric study centers, may be places where you can find information about in-person Gnostic study groups or people interested in forming a group. Ask the staff, check the bulletin boards, or participate in events promoted by these places.

Personal Initiative: Creating a Study Group: If the search for in-person Gnostic communities in your area is unsuccessful, consider the possibility of starting your own Gnostic study group. Start with friends, acquaintances, or people you find online who share your interest in Gnosticism. Organize regular meetings for reading and discussing Gnostic texts, joint meditative practices, or simply to share experiences and reflections on the spiritual journey.

Benefits of Sharing the Journey in Community:

Validation and Understanding: Feeling validated and understood in your spiritual search by other seekers who share similar perspectives.

Exchange of Knowledge and Experiences: Learning from the wisdom and experience of others, broadening the understanding of Gnosticism and enriching personal practice.

Emotional and Practical Support: Receiving support, encouragement, and assistance in challenging moments of the spiritual journey.

Motivation and Inspiration: Feeling motivated and inspired by the energy and enthusiasm of other seekers.

Sense of Belonging: Experiencing a sense of belonging to a spiritual community that shares similar values and aspirations.

Accelerated Spiritual Growth: Benefiting from the synergy and collective energy of the group to deepen practice and accelerate spiritual growth.

Respect for Diversity and Individuality in the Gnostic Community:

It is essential that the Gnostic community, whether virtual or real, be a space of respect for the diversity of interpretations, practices, and individual experiences. Gnosticism, in its essence, values the personal search for Gnosis and the direct experience of the divine, recognizing the plurality of paths and the uniqueness of each seeker's journey. Within the Gnostic community, there must be room for different theological perspectives, different practical approaches, and different ways of expressing Gnostic spirituality. Open dialogue, mutual respect, tolerance, and the valuing of diversity are essential qualities for a healthy and enriching Gnostic community. The Gnostic community should not become a space of dogmatism, proselytism, or exclusion, but rather an environment of mutual learning, fraternal support, and celebration of the spiritual journey in its multiple manifestations. Unity in diversity, the joint search, and respect for the individuality of each seeker must be the pillars of an authentic and vibrant Gnostic community.

Chapter 25
Deepening the Connection

The spiritual connection with Barbelo and the Pleroma is not established as an isolated event or a static experience, but as a continuous flow of expanding consciousness and deepening into the divine essence. Each step taken on this journey represents not only an advance, but the revelation of new layers of knowledge and perception, leading the seeker to an increasingly refined understanding of their spiritual nature. The call to this deepening is not an external imposition, but rather an inner yearning, an impulse of the soul that recognizes its origin in the primordial light and seeks incessantly to return to it. As this journey unfolds, it becomes evident that Gnostic spirituality is not a fixed set of dogmas or rigidly established practices, but a living, dynamic, and constantly transforming process, shaped by the direct experience of the sacred and by the evolution of the consciousness of the one who treads this path.

Progression in the connection with Barbelo involves transcending the limitations imposed by the conditioned mind and opening to higher states of perception and understanding. Unlike purely intellectual knowledge, Gnosis cannot be acquired solely through the study of sacred texts or the memorization of philosophical concepts; it is revealed through direct experience, confident surrender to mystery, and a willingness to explore more subtle dimensions of existence. This deepening demands not only discipline and perseverance, but also flexibility and receptivity, as each stage of the journey brings with it unexpected challenges and transformative insights. The true Gnostic seeker understands that there is no absolute end to be reached, for each revelation leads to new questions, each illumination unveils an even vaster horizon, and each integration of the sacred into everyday life paves the way for an even deeper connection with the Divine Source.

By accepting this journey as a continuous process, the Gnostic practitioner aligns with the cyclical and expansive nature of spiritual existence. The connection with Barbelo and the Pleroma is not limited to specific moments of meditation or contemplation, but intertwines with all aspects of life, shaping perceptions, inspiring actions, and nourishing the soul with the light of divine knowledge. Deepening this bond means not only seeking elevated states of consciousness, but also allowing that light to illuminate the most common aspects of existence, bringing clarity, purpose, and harmony to everyday life. In this way, spiritual practice becomes an integrated experience, where every experience, challenge, and discovery is seen as an opportunity for growth and expansion. The ultimate call of this journey is not to an end, but to a constant beginning, where each step taken opens doors to new mysteries and each awakening leads to an even deeper understanding of the divine essence that dwells within each being.

Recognizing spiritual practice as a continuous path of growth and deepening implies abandoning the illusion that there is a final state of enlightenment or a definitive point of arrival on the Gnostic journey. The Pleroma, the realm of perfection and fullness, is not a geographical destination to be reached, but rather a dimension of reality that manifests progressively in our consciousness as we deepen our connection with the Divine Source. The spiritual journey is not a race to reach a final point, but rather a continuous dance between the human soul and the divine, an ascending spiral of learning, transformation, and expansion of consciousness that unfolds throughout life. At each stage of the journey, new levels of depth are revealed, new horizons expand, and new mysteries present themselves, inviting us to move forward with enthusiasm and perseverance.

Encouraging the reader to continue exploring and expanding their connection with Barbelo and the Pleroma becomes a central objective of this final chapter. Gnostic spiritual practices, such as meditation, prayer, contemplation, visualization, and adapted rituals, are not techniques to be mastered and abandoned, but rather valuable tools to be used and continuously improved throughout the journey. Deepening the connection with Barbelo implies cultivating a living and dynamic relationship with the first emanation of the Divine Mind, exploring the multiple facets of her energy, wisdom, and love, and seeking her intuitive guidance in all areas of life. Expanding the connection with the Pleroma means opening oneself increasingly to spiritual reality, transcending the limitations of ordinary perception and allowing the divine light to illuminate and transform our consciousness in its totality.

The deepening of Gnostic spiritual practice can manifest in various ways. It may involve exploring new meditative techniques, improving visualization practices and channeling divine light, creating increasingly personal and authentic prayers and invocations, experimenting with more elaborate adapted rituals, or seeking new forms of creative expression inspired by Gnostic wisdom. Deepening can also manifest in the continuous study of Gnostic texts, reflection on their teachings, and the pursuit of an ever-deeper understanding of Gnostic cosmology, theology, and ethics. The important thing is to keep an open mind, a burning curiosity, and a clear intention to move forward on the journey, exploring new paths and deepening the spiritual experience.

The expansion of consciousness, as a natural result of continuous spiritual practice, represents a profound and comprehensive transformation of our way of perceiving reality and relating to the world. As we deepen our connection with Barbelo and the Pleroma, our perception becomes more subtle, more intuitive, and more comprehensive, transcending the limitations of the rational mind and the physical senses. Awakened consciousness recognizes the interconnectedness of all beings, the presence of divinity in all manifestations of life, and the spiritual reality that permeates the material universe. The expansion of consciousness is not an isolated event, but rather a gradual and continuous process, which unfolds throughout the spiritual journey, transforming our worldview, our values, and our way of life.

Openness to new discoveries and spiritual experiences throughout the journey constitutes a fundamental attitude for the Gnostic seeker. The spiritual path is not a predefined script or a set of inflexible dogmas, but rather an adventure of constant exploration and discovery. Keeping an open mind means abandoning prejudices, rigid expectations, and limiting beliefs, allowing spiritual experience to surprise us and lead us to unknown territories. Being open to new experiences means embracing uncertainty, welcoming mystery, and trusting the wisdom of intuition as guides on the journey. Spiritual discoveries can arise in unexpected ways, in moments of deep meditation, in meaningful encounters, in intuitive insights, or in seemingly banal everyday experiences. Being attentive and receptive to these discoveries, integrating them into our understanding and spiritual practice, enriches the journey and propels our growth.

The joy and beauty of the spiritual quest and connection with the divine emerge as intrinsic rewards of the Gnostic journey. The spiritual quest, in its essence, is not a heavy burden or an arduous duty, but rather a passionate adventure, full of moments of beauty, inspiration, and profound joy. The connection with Barbelo and the Pleroma nourishes the soul, illuminates the mind, and fills the heart with love, peace, and contentment. The joy of the spiritual quest lies in the continuous discovery of one's own divine nature, in the blossoming of the highest spiritual potential, and in living a life with more meaning, purpose, and fulfillment. The beauty of the connection with the divine manifests in the perception of cosmic harmony, in the contemplation of the vastness of mystery, and in the experience of the essential unity that permeates all creation. The Gnostic spiritual journey, in its deepest essence, is a celebration of life, light, and love, a path of return to home and awakening to the transcendent beauty that resides within us and throughout the universe.

May this book, "Barbelo: The Mystery of the First Emanation," serve as an initial map and an inspiring guide for your Gnostic spiritual journey. May the reflections, practices, and invocations presented here help you to begin or deepen your connection with Barbelo, the Supreme Mother, and the Pleroma. Remember that the journey is yours, unique and personal. Explore with curiosity, practice with devotion, trust your intuition, and embrace the adventure of awakening with courage and joy. May the light of Barbelo illuminate your path and may the love of the Supreme Mother sustain you in every step of the Continuing Journey. May Gnosis flourish in your heart and may the Peace of the Pleroma always be with you.

Chapter 26
Model for Inner Transformation

Inner transformation is a profound calling that resonates in the essence of every human being, urging the soul to transcend its limitations and reconnect with its divine origin. In the context of the Gnostic tradition, this journey of self-discovery and awakening is not just a psychological or philosophical process, but a spiritual quest that reflects the movement of creation itself towards its supreme principle. Barbelo, the first emanation of the Divine Source, symbolizes this archetypal principle of the soul in its fullness, manifesting as the perfect model for those who aspire to enlightenment and return to primordial unity. The figure of Barbelo represents both the origin and the destination of the inner journey, guiding the seeker through her light, wisdom, and creative power. Understanding this emanation not only as a cosmic concept, but as a reflection of one's own human nature, paves the way for a genuine transformation, in which the soul recognizes its luminous essence and assumes its role as co-author of its own spiritual evolution.

The journey towards inner transformation requires more than mere intellectual contemplation; it demands active engagement and the willingness to traverse the veils of illusion and forgetfulness. Barbelo, as the archetype of the awakened soul, offers a model for this crossing, demonstrating that awakening is not a sudden and isolated event, but a continuous process of integration and expansion of consciousness. The Gnostic path, sustained by the pursuit of Gnosis—the direct knowledge of spiritual reality—provides the tools for this journey, allowing the individual to recognize the influences that obscure their inner light and transcend them through wisdom and spiritual practice. This process does not occur without challenges, as it requires the deconstruction of limiting patterns and the reintegration of fragmented aspects of the self. However, by looking at Barbelo as a mirror, the seeker finds not only inspiration, but also strength and courage to persevere on the path of self-transformation.

The practical application of this archetypal model in everyday life manifests in the need to balance the complementary principles that make up the totality of being. Barbelo embodies the unity of the divine masculine and feminine, demonstrating that wholeness is only achieved when both forces are in harmony. Thus, inner transformation requires the individual to recognize and integrate these aspects within themselves, balancing reason and intuition, action and contemplation, strength and compassion. This balance is reflected in a more conscious life, where every thought, word, and action are aligned with spiritual truth and the soul's highest purpose. In this way, Barbelo not only illuminates the path of transformation, but also becomes a living and dynamic presence in the seeker's journey, guiding them in the reconquest of their primordial light and the manifestation of their divine potential in all dimensions of existence.

Barbelo, in her archetypal essence, represents the human soul in its primordial state of purity, potentiality, and connection with the Divine Source. Just as Barbelo emerges from the ineffable transcendence of the Ineffable Father, the divine spark within us yearns to awaken and manifest its innate light, freeing itself from the illusions of the material world and returning to its original fullness. The archetype of Barbelo invites us to recognize this divine potential within ourselves, to awaken the dormant consciousness, and to walk the path of individuation, becoming more complete, conscious beings aligned with our highest spiritual purpose.

The inspiration and encouragement that Barbelo offers for personal transformation reside in her own attributes and her function within Gnostic cosmology. Barbelo, as Divine Wisdom, inspires us to seek the knowledge that liberates, the Gnosis that reveals our true nature and the path of return to the Pleroma. Barbelo, as Divine Creative Power, encourages us to manifest our potential, to express our talents, and to co-create a reality more aligned with light and love. Barbelo, as Divine Immortality, offers us the hope of transcending death and the illusion of separation, pointing to eternal life and union with the Primordial Source as our ultimate destiny. By contemplating the archetype of Barbelo, we are imbued with courage, motivation, and confidence to face the challenges of the inner journey and persevere in the quest for awakening.

The journey towards wholeness and the integration of the inner feminine and masculine aspects finds in Barbelo a particularly relevant archetypal model. Barbelo, as "Mother-Father," personifies the primordial union of the feminine and masculine principles within the heart of divinity. In our journey of individuation, we are invited to recognize and integrate these two aspects in our own being, balancing the rational mind and intuition, action and receptivity, strength and tenderness, logos and eros. The archetype of Barbelo shows us that wholeness does not reside in polarization or the exclusion of one of the principles, but rather in their harmonization and integration, creating a more complete, balanced being capable of expressing the fullness of their divine nature. Honoring the archetype of Barbelo in our inner journey implies valuing and cultivating both our feminine and masculine aspects, recognizing the importance of both for our wholeness and well-being.

Barbelo, as the archetype of the awakened soul, emerges as a symbol of hope and potential for humanity as a whole. In a world often marked by suffering, division, and the incessant pursuit of material power and recognition, the archetype of Barbelo offers us an alternative vision, a path of return to our divine essence and of building a more just, compassionate, and enlightened world. Barbelo reminds us that true wealth does not reside in material goods or external power, but rather in inner light, in the knowledge that liberates, and in the love that unites. By internalizing the archetype of Barbelo, we become agents of transformation in our world, radiating the light of awakened consciousness, promoting compassion and justice, and contributing to the construction of a reality more aligned with the Pleroma. Barbelo, as the archetype of the awakened soul, invites us to awaken to our divine potential and to co-create a brighter future for humanity.

Reflections for the Inner Journey with the Archetype of Barbelo:

Meditation on the Archetype: Set aside time to meditate on the archetype of Barbelo, visualizing her image, contemplating her attributes, and seeking to feel her presence within you. Allow the archetype of Barbelo to inspire your journey of personal transformation.

Dialogue with the Archetype: Dialogue with the archetype of Barbelo through active imagination, intuitive writing, or oracle. Ask Barbelo about your challenges, your yearnings, and your next steps on the spiritual journey. Be open to receiving her intuitive guidance and ancestral wisdom.

Integration of Attributes: Seek to integrate Barbelo's attributes into your daily life. Cultivate wisdom in your decisions, manifest your creative power in your actions, express unconditional love in your relationships, and seek spiritual immortality through your Gnostic practice.

Honor the Inner Divine Feminine: Recognize and honor the Divine Feminine within your own being, cultivating intuition, receptivity, compassion, and creativity. Allow the feminine aspect of your nature to flourish and manifest fully.

Balance of Principles: Seek the balance and integration of the feminine and masculine principles in your life, harmonizing the rational mind and intuition, action and receptivity, logos and eros. Cultivate wholeness and completeness in your being, drawing inspiration from the androgynous archetype of Barbelo.

Barbelo, as the archetype of the awakened soul, is not just a distant divine figure, but rather a living and inspiring presence within us, a model for our personal transformation and a symbol of hope for humanity. By connecting with this powerful archetype, we awaken the divine spark within our being, strengthen our spiritual journey, and become agents of light and transformation in the world. May the archetype of Barbelo illuminate your path and inspire you to live the fullness of your divine potential.

Chapter 27
Western Spirituality

Western spirituality, in its long and multifaceted trajectory, has been shaped by diverse influences, some explicit and institutionalized, others subtle and subterranean. Among these currents, Gnosticism stands out as a tradition that, despite having been marginalized and combatted by the major organized religions, continued to exert a profound impact on the way the West understands the relationship between the human and the divine. The figure of Barbelo, as the first emanation of the Supreme Source and manifestation of the Divine Feminine, represents an essential link in this spiritual legacy, resonating through the ages as a symbol of transcendent knowledge and the quest for inner awakening. Her presence in Gnostic texts, especially in writings such as the Apocryphon of John, attests to her importance within ancient Gnostic schools, but her influence transcends these circles, manifesting in a veiled way in various mystical, philosophical, and spiritual currents that shaped the Western tradition.

The continuity of Gnostic thought, and with it the persistence of the archetypes that structure its cosmology, can be identified in different movements throughout history. Despite the persecution and attempted eradication of Gnostic teachings by orthodox Christian institutions, fundamental elements of this tradition survived, whether through Hermeticism, medieval alchemy, Renaissance mysticism, or modern esoteric movements. The idea of a secret knowledge that leads to the liberation of the soul and the notion of a corrupted material world, which must be transcended through Gnosis, reappear in different contexts and eras, always offering a counterpoint to dominant doctrines. The image of Barbelo, as the celestial mother and source of true wisdom, can be traced in these traditions, often under other names and forms, but always carrying the same essence: the promise of a return to the primordial light.

In contemporary times, the rediscovery of Gnostic texts and the growing interest in the Divine Feminine have brought Barbelo back to the center of spiritual reflections. The rediscovery of the Nag Hammadi library in the 20th century allowed these forgotten traditions to be reexamined and reinterpreted, offering an alternative to traditional forms of religiosity. The resurgence of interest in Gnosticism, especially within esoteric circles and the New Age movement, reflects a collective search for a more experiential spirituality, less dogmatic and more connected to the intuitive and feminine dimensions of the sacred. In this context, Barbelo re-emerges as an inspiring figure for those who seek not only to understand spirituality intellectually, but to experience it as a continuous process of transformation and return to the divine essence. Thus, her legacy persists, crossing the centuries and adapting to new forms of spiritual seeking, always evoking the eternal journey of the soul towards the light.

Throughout the history of Gnosticism, from its origins in the ancient world to its most recent manifestations, the figure of Barbelo has maintained a position of prominence and reverence. In various Gnostic schools, such as Sethianism, Valentinianism, and other lesser-known currents, Barbelo is consistently presented as the first emanation, the perfect image of the Ineffable Father, the primordial Divine Mother, and the source of wisdom and light. In the Nag Hammadi texts, such as the Apocryphon of John, the Gospel of the Egyptians, and the Thought of Norea, Barbelo is invoked, praised, and described with a variety of epithets that exalt her greatness and her fundamental role in Gnostic cosmology. Whether as "the First Thought," "the Image of the Father," or "the Virgin Light," Barbelo remains a constant in the Gnostic pantheon, witnessing the enduring importance of the Divine Feminine and the pursuit of Gnosis as paths of return to the divine.

The legacy of Barbelo within Gnosticism manifests in the continuity of her veneration and the persistence of her attributes over time. In different schools and texts, we find variations in cosmology and mythical narratives, but the central figure of Barbelo as the first emanation, endowed with wisdom, creative power, and immortality, remains constant. This consistency suggests that Barbelo was not just a mere mythological character, but rather an archetypal representation of an essential dimension of divinity, an aspect of the Divine Feminine that resonated deeply with Gnostic seekers of different eras and contexts. The legacy of Barbelo in Gnosticism is a legacy of persistence, of continuous relevance, and of profound impact on the Gnostic spiritual imagination.

The influence of Gnosticism, and by extension, of the archetype of Barbelo, on the history of Western spirituality is a complex and multifaceted theme, subject to debate and academic investigation. Although there is no direct evidence of an uninterrupted "line of succession" between ancient Gnosticism and later spiritual currents, thematic resonances and parallels suggest possible influences, direct or indirect, of Gnostic thought on various Western spiritual and philosophical traditions. It is important to approach this topic with nuance and caution, avoiding generalized or simplistic statements, but recognizing the possible connections and the remarkable similarities that emerge from comparative analysis.

Possible areas of influence of Gnosticism, which deserve consideration, include:

Hermeticism: The Corpus Hermeticum, a set of philosophical-religious texts from the late Hellenistic period, shares several characteristics with Gnosticism, such as the emphasis on spiritual knowledge (Gnosis), the view of an imperfect material world, and the pursuit of the divinization of the soul. Although the exact origins of Hermeticism are complex and debated, it is possible that there were mutual influences or common sources between Hermeticism and some Gnostic currents, including the valorization of androgynous divine figures and the search for transcendent knowledge.

Kabbalah: The Jewish mysticism of Kabbalah, in its medieval and later manifestations, presents some similarities with Gnostic cosmology, such as the idea of divine emanations (Sephirot), the hierarchy of spiritual worlds, and the pursuit of union with the divine. Although Kabbalah has its roots in rabbinic Judaism, some scholars suggest that there may have been Gnostic influences, direct or indirect, in the formation of certain Kabbalistic concepts and symbols, especially in relation to the Kabbalistic Sophia, which shares some similarities with the Gnostic Sophia and, by extension, with Barbelo as a manifestation of Divine Wisdom.

Christian Mysticism: Although orthodox Christianity distanced itself from and condemned Gnosticism as heresy, some Christian mystical currents, especially in the medieval and Renaissance periods, manifested resonances with Gnostic themes, such as the pursuit of the direct experience of God, the valorization of intuition and inner knowledge, and a certain tension with dogmatic and institutionalized theology. Figures like Meister Eckhart, Jacob Boehme, and some Renaissance mystics may have been influenced, directly or indirectly, by Gnostic ideas, although these influences are often complex and subtle. It is important to note that this area is sensitive and subject to different theological interpretations.

Philosophy of the Renaissance and Romanticism: The Renaissance, with its interest in ancient philosophy and Hermetic texts, and Romanticism, with its valorization of intuition, imagination, and subjective experience, created a cultural climate more receptive to ideas that resonate with Gnosticism. Renaissance philosophers like Marsilio Ficino and Pico della Mirandola, and Romantic poets and thinkers like William Blake and some exponents of German idealism, manifested interest in themes such as primordial unity, the pursuit of transcendent knowledge, and the critique of purely instrumental reason, themes that can be associated, albeit indirectly, with some strands of Gnostic thought.

Modern Spirituality and New Age: The New Age movement and contemporary modern spirituality manifest a growing interest in Gnosticism, reinterpreting and re-signifying Gnostic concepts such as Gnosis, the inner light, the Divine Feminine, and the pursuit of the direct experience of the divine. The rediscovery of the Nag Hammadi texts in the 20th century and the growing criticism of traditional religious institutions contributed to this renewed interest in Gnosticism, seen by many as an alternative source of spirituality, more focused on personal experience, freedom of thought, and the valorization of the divine feminine. In this context, Barbelo, as an archetype of the Divine Feminine, re-emerges with force, inspiring contemporary spiritual seekers in their journey of self-discovery and connection with the sacred.

The rediscovery of Gnosticism and the divine feminine principle in the contemporary era represents a significant phenomenon in the history of Western spirituality. The finding of the Nag Hammadi library in

1945 and the subsequent translation and dissemination of Gnostic texts opened a new horizon for the understanding of ancient Gnosticism and for its reappropriation in the modern context. This rediscovery coincided with the growth of feminist movements, the critique of patriarchal structures, and the yearning for forms of spirituality that value the feminine, the intuitive, and the experiential. In this scenario, Gnosticism, with its emphasis on the Divine Feminine, in figures like the Supreme Mother and Barbelo, and on the pursuit of Gnosis as a path of liberation and empowerment, re-emerged as a relevant and inspiring spiritual tradition for many contemporary seekers.

The relevance of the Supreme Mother and the divine feminine for the contemporary world lies in its ability to offer a counterpoint to the dominant patriarchal religious traditions, which have often marginalized or silenced the feminine aspect of divinity. In a world that yearns for balance, harmony, and a more integral vision of reality, the rescue of the Divine Feminine, exemplified in figures like Barbelo, represents an important step towards the healing of the collective psyche and the construction of a more equitable and spiritually rich future. The archetype of Barbelo, as a symbol of the awakened soul and the integration of the feminine and masculine principles, offers an inspiring model for personal transformation and for the construction of a more just, compassionate, and enlightened world.

The importance of preserving and studying the Gnostic legacy for future generations lies in the wealth of insights and perspectives that this spiritual tradition offers for the existential and spiritual questions that humanity faces. Gnosticism, with its pursuit of Gnosis, its critique of materialism, its valorization of inner experience, and its vision of an interconnected universe, continues to resonate with the yearnings and anxieties of contemporary human beings. Preserving and studying the Gnostic legacy, including the luminous figure of Barbelo, means keeping alive a source of ancestral wisdom that can illuminate our path, challenge our limiting conceptions, and inspire our journey of awakening and transformation. The legacy of Barbelo, as an archetype of the Divine Feminine and the awakened soul, is a spiritual treasure that deserves to be preserved, studied, and transmitted to future generations, as a beacon of hope and an invitation to the incessant pursuit of truth and light.

Chapter 28
Other Emanations

The Pleroma, brimming with light and knowledge, is not limited to a single emanation, but expands into a complex network of divine beings, each reflecting distinct aspects of the Supreme Source. Barbelo, the First Emanation, occupies a central place in Gnostic cosmology, but her splendor does not exist in isolation. Around her, a myriad of other Aeons unfolds, forming a vibrant fabric of wisdom, love, and spiritual power. These Aeons, emanated from the divine fullness, play fundamental roles in the process of creation, enlightenment, and redemption of souls seeking to return to their original state of unity with the divine. Understanding these emanations is to delve into the mystical structure of the Gnostic universe, exploring how the divine manifests in different dimensions and interacts with human existence.

Each Aeon carries within it an essential attribute of the Supreme Source, functioning as a channel between the divine and creation. While Barbelo symbolizes primordial purity and divine intelligence, other emanations express themselves as complementary forces that sustain and harmonize the spiritual cosmos. The Logos, often identified with Christ in Gnosticism, is the manifestation of the Creative Word, the one who brings order and reason to the universe. Sophia, Wisdom, represents both the longing for truth and the risk of separation from the divine, reflecting the dilemma of the human soul that oscillates between light and matter. Beyond these, an infinity of other emanations make up the structure of the Pleroma, serving as guides, guardians, and revealers of Gnosis. The study of these sacred entities allows us to glimpse the magnitude of divine creation and understand the journey of the spirit in search of reintegration with the totality.

By entering this complex network of emanations, the Gnostic seeker realizes that every aspect of the divine is reflected within themselves. The Pleroma is not only a distant realm of luminous beings, but also a map for understanding one's own human essence. Just as the divine emanations express facets of the Creator, each soul contains within it the spark of these qualities and the potential to awaken to its true nature. By exploring the emanations of the Pleroma, we not only broaden our understanding of Gnostic cosmology, but also find keys to our own spiritual transformation. Each Aeon, with its light and wisdom, invites us to look within, to recognize our divine origin, and to walk the path back to the Source, guided by Gnosis and the longing for transcendence.

The Pleroma, as we have already explored, is not an empty or homogeneous space, but rather a dynamic and hierarchical realm, populated by numerous divine emanations, the Aeons, each with its specific qualities, attributes, and functions. Although Barbelo occupies the place of primacy as the first emanation, countless other Aeons emerge from the Divine Source, contributing to the complexity and richness of the Pleroma. Presenting some of these Aeons and important figures is essential to understand the vastness of Gnostic cosmology and the diversity of divine manifestations.

Presentation of Other Aeons and Important Figures of the Pleroma (besides Barbelo):

Christ (Logos): In many Gnostic schools, Christ is considered an important Aeon, often identified with the Logos, the Divine Word, and with the Divine Son. Christ is seen as an emissary of the Pleroma sent to the material world to awaken the sleeping humanity and reveal the path of Gnosis and redemption. His function is to help human souls recognize their divine origin and return to the realm of light.

Sophia (Wisdom): Sophia, whose name means "Wisdom" in Greek, is another essential Aeon figure in Gnosticism, often associated with passion, suffering, and the search for restoration. In some Gnostic cosmologies, Sophia's fall from the Pleroma, driven by a desire to create without the permission of the Divine Source, is the primordial event that leads to the creation of the imperfect material world. Sophia represents Divine Wisdom in its quest for redemption and reunification with the Pleroma.

Set (Seth): Seth, the third son of Adam and Eve in the biblical tradition, is revered in some Gnostic schools, especially in Sethianism, as a divine emanation and a spiritual ancestor of the Gnostic lineage. Seth is seen as a being of light who possesses the knowledge of truth and who transmits Gnosis to his spiritual descendants. His figure represents the continuity of the divine lineage in the material world and the promise of redemption for those who follow the path of Gnosis.

The Luminous Christ (Jesus): In Gnosticism, the figure of Jesus Christ is reinterpreted and resignified, distancing itself from the orthodox Christian view. For Gnostics, Jesus is not the only begotten Son of God incarnated in the flesh, but rather an emissary of the Pleroma, an enlightened being who manifested the Cosmic Christ (the Aeon Logos) and who came to the world to awaken Gnosis in human souls. The Gnostic Christ is a spiritual master, a revealer of truth, and a guide to the path of liberation.

The Holy Spirit (Pneuma Hagion): The Holy Spirit, in the Gnostic perspective, is understood as the divine force that animates creation, that inspires Gnosis, and that leads souls towards the Pleroma. The Holy Spirit is not a divine person distinct from the Primordial Source, but rather a manifestation of its energy and presence in the universe. The Holy Spirit is the force that drives the awakening of consciousness and spiritual ascension.

The Demiurge (Yaldabaoth, Saklas, etc.): In contrast to the luminous Aeons of the Pleroma, the Demiurge represents the ignorant and imperfect creative force that generated the material world. The Demiurge, often identified with the God of the Old Testament, is seen as an inferior emanation, blind to the truth of the Pleroma and responsible for the creation of a world of illusion, suffering, and ignorance. Understanding the nature of the Demiurge and his role in Gnostic cosmology is essential to understanding the Gnostic view of the origin of evil and the need for spiritual redemption.

The vastness and complexity of Gnostic cosmology reflect the search to understand the nature of the divine and the origin of the universe in its totality. The hierarchy of the Aeons, the dynamic between the Pleroma and the material world, the interaction between the forces of light and darkness, are themes that challenge our rational mind and invite us to contemplation and intuition. Gnostic cosmology does not present itself as a dogmatic and inflexible system, but rather as a symbolic map, an archetypal language that seeks to express the unfathomable mystery of divine reality. Exploring Gnostic cosmology involves diving into an ocean of symbols, myths, and metaphors, allowing our mind to expand beyond the limitations of linear thinking and open itself to the vastness of the spiritual universe.

The invitation to the reader to continue exploring the mysteries of the Pleroma and the Gnostic universe is a call to the adventure of the soul, an endless journey in search of knowledge, wisdom, and connection with the divine. This book has offered only a glimpse of the richness and depth of Gnosticism, and the exploration of Barbelo is only a starting point for a much broader investigation. The Gnostic universe is vast and inexhaustible, full of texts, symbols, practices, and teachings that can enrich our spiritual journey and expand our consciousness in unimaginable ways. The Gnostic quest is a personal and unique journey for each seeker, and the invitation is for each reader to follow their own path, exploring the mysteries of the Pleroma with curiosity, discernment, and an open heart.

Suggestions for Readings and Resources to Deepen the Study of Gnosticism:

For those who wish to continue exploring the Gnostic universe and deepen their knowledge, we suggest some resources and readings that may be valuable:

Gnostic Texts of Nag Hammadi: The direct reading of the Gnostic texts of Nag Hammadi is fundamental for an authentic and deep understanding of Gnosticism. There are several translations available, including academic editions and more accessible translations for the general public. Texts such as the Apocryphon of John, the Gospel of Thomas, the Gospel of Mary Magdalene, the Gospel of Philip, and the Sacred Book of the Great Invisible Spirit are just a few examples of the richness and diversity of Gnostic texts.

Introductory Books to Gnosticism: For those who wish to begin the study of Gnosticism, there are several introductory books that offer an overview of Gnostic history, cosmology, theology, and practices. The book "Gnosticism" by Kurt Rudolph, "The Secret Book of the Gnostics" by Jean Doresse and "Gnosticism: A Historical Introduction" by Nicola Denzey Lewis, are some valuable books about the subject.

Academic Studies on Gnosticism: For a more in-depth and rigorous study of Gnosticism, there are numerous academic studies and research articles produced by specialists in Gnosticism and ancient religions. Specialized academic journals, books of collected articles, and reference works can be found in university libraries and online academic research platforms.

Websites and Online Communities on Gnosticism: The internet offers a vast array of online resources on Gnosticism, including websites, blogs, forums, and virtual communities dedicated to the study and practice of Gnosticism. It is important to discern online sources, looking for websites and communities that are based on academic sources and informed interpretations of Gnosticism, avoiding superficial or sensationalist New Age approaches.

Gnostic Study and Practice Groups: Participating in study groups or Gnostic communities, whether in person or online, can enrich the learning journey and offer a space for sharing, discussion, and mutual support with other seekers. The exchange of ideas, the sharing of experiences, and joint practice can deepen understanding and strengthen the experience of Gnostic spirituality.

Exploring the Pleroma and the mysteries of the Gnostic universe is a lifelong journey, an adventure of the soul that invites us to transcend the limits of the mind and open the heart to the vastness of the divine. May your journey of exploration continue to be illuminated by the light of Gnosis and guided by the wisdom of Barbelo and the Pleroma. May the incessant search for truth and light lead you to increasingly profound and transformative discoveries. The Gnostic universe, in its infinite expansion, awaits your exploration, full of mysteries, challenges, and countless spiritual blessings. Go forward with courage, curiosity, and the certainty that the journey itself is the greatest reward.

Chapter 29
Returning to the Source

The return to the Source is not a simple movement of arrival at a final destination, but a cyclical and continuous journey, in which the seeker rediscovers, at each step, the deep connection between their essence and divine fullness. Within the Gnostic tradition, this journey is not just a search for intellectual knowledge, but a living process of inner transformation, a progressive awakening of consciousness that leads the soul back to its original state of unity with the divine. Barbelo, as the First Emanation, symbolizes this primordial link between the Creator and creation, representing the light that guides the spirit along this crossing. However, the journey does not end in the contemplation of this supreme emanation; on the contrary, it extends beyond conceptual understanding, inviting each seeker to integrate this wisdom into their own existence, becoming a living reflection of the light that once seemed lost, but always resided in their being. Along this quest for the return to the Source, the challenge lies not only in obtaining Gnosis, but in its incorporation into daily life. True awakening does not happen only in moments of contemplation or study, but in the way each individual expresses their inner light in the world. Gnostic practice teaches that the return to the Pleroma is not an escape from material reality, but a reconfiguration of perception, a profound change in the gaze that allows one to see the presence of the divine in all things. Living this wisdom implies transforming each experience into a learning, each interaction into an opportunity to expand consciousness, and each obstacle into a chance to refine the soul. The Gnostic path, therefore, is not defined only by the knowledge acquired, but by the way this knowledge manifests itself in everyday life, in choices, actions, and relationships that reflect the light of awakening.

In this way, the journey of return to the Source is, in its essence, a perpetual restart. Each step taken towards illumination reveals new mysteries, each unveiled layer of reality opens the way for even deeper understandings. The call of Barbelo, of the Supreme Mother and of the Pleroma, is not an invitation to a definitive end, but to a continuous movement of spiritual expansion and ascension. May this quest not end with the pages of this book, but perpetuate itself as a personal commitment to awakening, guiding each seeker to fully live their connection with the divine, bringing the light of the Pleroma to earthly experience and allowing Gnosis to flourish in every aspect of existence. Summarizing the main themes and learnings of the book is essential to consolidate the acquired knowledge and reinforce the central messages that permeate our entire exploration. Throughout the chapters, we navigated the history and characteristics of Gnosticism, explored Gnostic cosmology and the hierarchy of the Aeons, delved into the mystery of Barbelo as the First Emanation and the archetype of the Divine Feminine, understood the importance of divine light as the essence of spiritual reality, and unveiled practices for connection, overcoming obstacles, and integrating Gnostic wisdom into everyday life. Remembering these main themes allows us to internalize the teachings, strengthen our understanding, and inspire the continuation of spiritual practice. We reaffirm the importance of connection with Barbelo, the Supreme Mother, and the divine light as the beating heart of the Gnostic journey. Barbelo, as the first manifestation of the Divine Source and the archetype of the Divine Feminine, emerges as a luminous guide, a bridge between the human and the divine, a model for the awakened soul. The Supreme Mother, as the primordial Source from which everything emanates, represents the divine feminine principle in its totality, the cosmic matrix, and the source of unconditional love. Divine light, as the essence of spiritual reality, constitutes the path of return to the Pleroma, the transforming force that illuminates consciousness, heals wounds, and awakens our divine potential. Cultivating connection with Barbelo, the Supreme Mother, and the divine light is not just a spiritual practice, but a path to fullness, to wisdom, and to the love that nourishes the soul and transforms life.

The final message we wish to convey is a message of hope, inspiration, and encouragement for each reader on their unique and personal spiritual journey. The Gnostic path is not an easy or linear path, but it is a path of profound beauty, full of spiritual and transformative rewards. The search for Gnosis, the yearning for the awakening of consciousness, and the desire to return to the Source are noble and authentic impulses of the human soul. We believe in the potential of each individual to awaken their inner light, to connect with the divine, and to experience the fullness of their spiritual nature. May this book have served as a beacon, illuminating the first steps of your journey and offering an initial map for exploring the vast and mysterious territory of Gnosticism. We now invite the reader to continue to practice, explore, and live Gnostic wisdom in their daily life. Spiritual practice is not limited to formal moments of meditation or ritual, but extends to all areas of our existence. Living Gnostic wisdom implies cultivating mindfulness, compassion, truth, and service to others in all our actions and relationships. It implies seeking the knowledge that liberates, expanding our perception of reality, and awakening intuition as an inner guide. It implies honoring the Divine Feminine in ourselves and in the world, recognizing the importance of balance, harmony, and the integration of feminine and masculine principles. The Gnostic journey is a journey to be lived in its entirety, with courage, curiosity, and joy, in each moment of the present, in each step of the way.

May the light of Barbelo continue to illuminate your path, revealing the mysteries of the Pleroma and guiding you towards Gnosis. May the love of the Supreme Mother embrace and sustain you, nourishing your soul and strengthening your perseverance. May the peace of the Pleroma always accompany you, radiating from within you to the outside world. May the journey of return to the Source manifest in your life as a continuous awakening of inner light, an expansion of consciousness, and an experience of divine fullness in every breath, in every heartbeat, in every step of the Continuous Journey.

Epilogue

The spiritual journey, as explored throughout these pages, is not a linear path, nor a fixed destination to be reached. It is an ascending spiral, a continuous process of awakening, expansion, and reintegration with the primordial light. The soul that dares to tread this path discovers that each answer reached opens new questions, each illumination reveals new mysteries, and each step towards truth brings with it an even deeper call to move forward. The figure of Barbelo, the First Emanation, accompanies us along this journey. She is not just a symbol, but a beacon, a living link between the human and the divine. She represents the wisdom, totality, and fullness of the Supreme Source, serving as a guide for those who feel the longing for return to the Pleroma. Her light reminds us that we are not isolated in our search; that there is a path to be trodden and a hidden truth waiting to be unveiled within each awakened being.

Throughout this work, we have entered the depths of the Gnostic tradition, explored its cosmology, and unveiled the mysteries of the Divine Feminine, represented in Barbelo as the cosmic matrix of creation. We have learned that Gnosis is not intellectual knowledge, but a transformative experience, a revelation that resonates in the deepest essence of the soul. To know is to become, to understand is to integrate, to awaken is to remember who we really are.

However, understanding Gnosis and recognizing the divine spark within oneself is not enough. The true challenge lies in integrating this wisdom into everyday life. What is the point of catching glimpses of the truth if we continue to live trapped in the illusions of the material world? The call of Gnosis is not an invitation to escape, but to the transmutation of earthly existence. Every thought, every choice, every action can become a reflection of the light of the Pleroma, an expression of the divine essence that dwells within us. To live spiritually is to transform one's own reality. It is to see the sacred in the ordinary, to recognize the divine in the flow of life, to transmute shadows into consciousness. The path of ascension does not take place in a parallel reality or in a distant future – it happens now, in the present, in the simple act of being awake and conscious. Each human being is a portal to the Pleroma, a mirror of divine light, and the spiritual journey consists of cleaning this mirror, of removing the layers of forgetfulness that obscure the true essence.

Thus, this book does not end here. The words were just a bridge, an invitation to the journey that each seeker must tread for themselves. The written pages can be read and reread, but true understanding will not come from the repetition of the text, but from the direct experience of Gnosis. This is just the beginning, a call to deepening, to practice, to the incorporation of light and wisdom in every breath, in every thought, and in every choice. May Barbelo, the Supreme Mother, continue to guide your journey. May her light illuminate the steps of those who seek the truth. May Gnosis flourish within you and may your awakening expand beyond the boundaries of illusion. The return to the Source is not an end – it is a perpetual rebirth, an eternal cycle of ascension and revelation. The search for truth does not end with this book, but is perpetuated in your consciousness, in your practice, and in your transformation. The journey continues.

www.ingramcontent.com/pod-product-compliance
Lightning Source LLC
LaVergne TN
LVHW040054080526
838202LV00045B/3624